Mountain Biking in Lakeland

by

Michael Hyde

"For Mags"

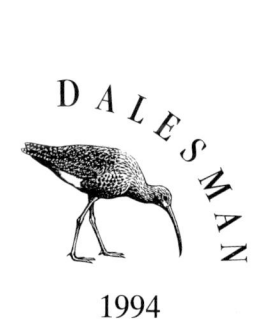

DALESMAN

1994

Dalesman Publishing Company Limited,
Stable Courtyard, Broughton Hall,
Skipton, North Yorkshire BD23 3AE

First Published 1988
This Edition 1994

Text © 1994 Michael Hyde
Cover photo by Eric Whitehead

Printed by The Grange Press

A British Library Cataloguing in Publication
record is available for this book

ISBN 1 85568 017 3

All rights reserved. This book must not be circulated in any form of binding or cover other than that in which it is published and without similar condition to this being imposed on the subsequent purchaser. No part of this publication may be reproduced, stored on a retrieval system or transmitted in any form, or by any means, electronic, mechanical, photocopying, recording or otherwise, without either prior permission in writing from the publisher or a licence permitting restricted copying. In the United Kingdom such licences are issued by the Copyright Licensing Agency, 90 Tottenham Court Road, London W1P 9HE. The right of Michael Hyde to be identified as the author of this work has been asserted by him in accordance with Copyright Designs and Patents Act 1988.

Contents

Introduction		5
1 Loughrigg from Ambleside	Grade 1	7
2 Claife Heights from Ambleside	Grade 2	11
3 Satterthwaite from Ambleside	Grade 3	15
4 Troutbeck from Ambleside	Grade 3	17
5 The Garburn Pass from Ambleside	Grade 4	21
6 Longsleddale from Kentmere	Grade 2	23
7 Grizedale Forest from Hawkshead	Grade 4	27
8 Langdale from Elterwater	Grade 1	31
9 Tarn Hows from Elterwater	Grade 2	35
10 Walna Scar Road from Coniston	Grade 5	37
11 Skiddaw House from Keswick	Grade 2	41
12 Moor Divock from Pooley Bridge	Grade 1	44
Cycle Hire Centres and Bike Shops		47
Bibliography		48

KEY TO MAPS

⫽	"OFF ROAD" ROUTE
───	ON ROAD
----	FOOTPATH
⊢#⊢	GATE; CATTLE GRID
⇉	VERY STEEP
=▷	LEADS TO
‖▷	ADJACENT ROUTE
⫽ ←RED→	FOREST CYCLE ROUTE
∽/↗	STREAM; BRIDGE
┼┼┼┼┼┼┼▫	RAILWAY; STATION
- - - -	COURSE OF OLD RAILWAY
╪	WALLS [IN COMPLEX AREAS ONLY]
♧ ♧	WOODLAND
⚡	ROCK FACE
▲ ⛺	YOUTH HOSTEL; CAMP SITE
②	CONTINUATION
⊙	SUMMIT CAIRN
⊥	SWAMP
◪	ORIENTEERING
▫	SETTLEMENT
✝	CHURCH
⚲→	CYCLE SHOP OR HIRE [SEE BACK OF BOOK]
⤢	NORTH POINTER

Enjoy cycling in the Lake District
A Code of Conduct

RIGHTS OF WAY – Where You Can Ride
Public Bridleways – open to cyclists, but you must give way to walkers and horseriders.
Public Byways – unsurfaced tracks open to cyclists, as well as walkers, horseriders and motor vehicles.
All public roads – some of which are not tarmaced.
Designated cycle paths – these may be found on Forestry Commission land, on disused railway lines and other open spaces. These should usually be signed.
Look out for finger posts from the highway (Public bridleway; Public byway). Some routes may be waymarked – blue arrows for a bridleway, red for a byway.

ACCESS RESTRICTIONS
Public footpaths – no right to cycle exists – these may be waymarked by yellow arrows.
Open land – on most upland, moorland and farmland cyclists normally have no right of access without express permission from the landowner.
Roadside pavements – cycling is not permitted on pavements.

ADVICE – Riding Tips
Carry sufficient equipment for you and your bike.
Ride safely and maintain control at all times.
Brake smoothly and progressively to avoid surface damage.
Please keep to the line of the track.
Avoid widening soft and boggy areas.
Avoid bunching up and obstructing a trail when riding in a group.
Please don't make undue noise.
You must give way to horses and walkers.
Be pleasant to other countryside users – getting angry never solves a problem.

ALWAYS FOLLOW THE COUNTRY CODE

Introduction

WHEN Neolithic man, living as he did on Cumbria's western coast, walked to work at the Langdale Axe Factory he created the first footpath over Sty Head. Since then, a complex network including Roman Roads, Packhorse Trails and Miners Tracks has developed in the heart of the Lake District. These routes make use of every available pass through the fells and even though their original purposes are long dead, they are still used today by countless thousands of hillwalkers. Many of those walkers never stop to consider the origins of these ancient ways or who, be it Roman legions from Hardknott, Monks from Furness Abbey or Miners from Coniston, trod the same path centuries before.

Now, with the advent of the "Mountain Bike", these historic routes are being crossed by yet another kind of traveller. The Mountain Bike with its low gears, fat tyres and laid back frame angles arrived in this country a little over four years ago from the States and it is now estimated that there are over 15,000 on Britain's streets. Occasionally some of these find their way on to the fells of the Lake District and it is for these enthusiasts that this book is written.

The title "Mountain Bike" is a bit of a misnomer for two reasons. The first being that in the Lakes only three mountains can be cycled up legally, High Street, Helvellyn and Skiddaw and the second is that such a route involves a great deal of hard work and usually a lot of picking up and carrying. "All Terrain Bike" is a better description. After all, why spend a vast amount of money on a bike to carry it up a mountain when there are hundreds of miles of dirt roads, forest tracks and bridleways waiting to be explored.

In addition to the maps and text in the following twelve chapters, an invaluable companion should be the 1:25000 Outdoor Leisure maps produced by the Ordnance Survey.

The twelve routes described in this book are in the main low level, circular affairs centred on the Ambleside/Windermere area with one or two each for Hawkshead/Coniston and Keswick. They are described in such a direction as to make the uphills as bearable and the downhills as exciting as possible but of course they may be reversed or combined to make longer journeys if desired. Other routes can be created by using the O.S. maps to find other bridleways but remember, ONLY bridleways may be cycled, NOT footpaths — don't get the sport a bad name!

The twelve routes have been graded from 1 to 5, taking into account the length in kilometres and "severity" in metres of climbing per kilometre. Grade 1 is mainly a gentle day out allowing plenty of time for visiting places en route. Route 10, Walna Scar which attains a grade 5 rating comprises a fairly full day's trip climbing to nearly 2000′ and requires a reasonable level of fitness and stamina. To get a comparative grade for alternative routes simply divide the distance in km by 8¾ and the severity in m/km by 7½, add the two together and subtract 3!

If you are considering tackling any of the routes which reach an altitude of 2000', remember the Lake District's weather is notorious for turning nasty at the drop of a hat. The same equipment should be carried as for a day on the hills, waterproofs, hat and gloves, spare jumper, etc. etc. and the local weather can be obtained on Windermere (09662) 5151. Helmets and tools are both a matter of personal choice. Finally a word of warning, Mountain Bikers are still regarded by some as a nuisance, so please respect other people's right to enjoy the Lake District; be especially courteous when approaching walkers from behind, give plenty of warning and remember some mountain bikes have exceptionally wide handlebars, so leave enough room. Above all, obey the country code, don't trespass — even if areas like Grizedale Forest do look like a giant playground — and have a good time!

1   Loughrigg

AS a first route, this is most suitable taking only a couple of hours (longer if Grasmere is included) and being fairly gentle in its gradients, although the initial climb from the village is a bit arduous!

Ambleside was first settled in AD 80 when at Waterhead Agricola built the small fort of "Galava" on the delta of the Rothay and Brathay rivers. It was an important point on what has been recognised as the Tenth Iter or route 10 in the official road atlas of the Roman Empire, that from Whitchurch near Chester to Ravenglass and would have held an infantry cohort of five hundred men. Apart from Galava, Ambleside has two other attractions. The Little House on the Bridge built in 1723 as a summerhouse and apple store in the grounds of Ambleside Hall and Stock Ghyll Force, a 70 foot waterfall behind the Salutation Inn.

Route 1 leaves Ambleside in the direction of Coniston but after crossing Rothay Bridge at the back of the village heads right, along the "Under Loughrigg" road. Just after the cattle grid a steep drive is signposted — to the fell — and this is where the fun begins. After climbing around a series of hairpins originally designed to ease the passage of laden packhorses bound for Elterwater the track finally eases and Pine Rigg is reached. This, believe it or not, was the club house of Ambleside's very own Golf Course, what a view to have from the 18th hole. Keeping the wall on the right, go through the top gate to reach the saddle at the top of the climb. It's a tricky manoeuvre to cross the stream without losing balance, the sharp right turn at the bottom loses all the momentum needed to get out of the other side. The way now follows the obvious track around the base of Ivy Crag to Tarn Foot and then along the lanes above Loughrigg Tarn to the top of Red Bank.

Now, to return to Ambleside, go through the gate opposite the Elterwater road and drop down through the National Trust's Deerbolt Woods to Loughrigg Terrace. As with many of the bridleways in the area it was once a packhorse route, this one from Elterwater to Rydal then Patterdale via High Sweden Bridge. It is now such a popular hiking path that on this section, more than any other in the book, you *must* be considerate of other people, especially as a fair speed can be attained on the way down to Rydal Water. At one point on the lake shore, the path goes around a rocky point and after heavy rain the water can be lapping round your ankles and wheel hubs! At the end of the lake, rejoin the Under Loughrigg road at Pelter Bridge and follow it back to Ambleside.

If you want to visit Grasmere descend Red Bank around the back of the lake to arrive in the village itself. As early as the thirteenth century, this stretch of road formed an important link between Hawkshead and Grange in Borrowdale, two of the estates of the then largest landowner in the area, the

Through the edge of Rydal Water. *(Mike Hyde)*

monks of Furness Abbey. Each autumn in Grange the monks would gather thousands of sheep from their pasture and drive them via Watendlath, Dunmail Raise and Red Bank to their Abbey Farm in Hawkshead. There they would have been joined by many more herded from Brotherilkeld in Eskdale over Hardknott, Wrynose and Arnside (see Route 8) to be counted before being sent south, collecting still more on the way to winter near the abbey on Walney Island.

Grasmere has received immortality by being home of the poet Wordsworth from 1799 to 1809, although before then it was a thriving village on the crossroads of trade routes from Borrowdale over Greenup Edge, Keswick via Dunmail Raise and Patterdale past Grisedale Tarn.

There is plenty to see and do in Grasmere but as you leave, go past St. Oswalds Church and cross the A591 to pass in front of Wordsworth's home, Dove Cottage. The present route of the main road along the edge of the lake was laid out in 1825 by the Ambleside Turnpike Trust (much to the annoyance of the Wordsworths who used to walk amongst the bluebells there) and replaced the steeper route over White Moss Common. At How Top where the road veers to the right a signpost points to "Rydal, unsuitable for motors". This is the sort of route we are looking for. The only difficulty to be encountered, apart from the number of gates, is where the path goes sharply downhill to the right of a large stone retaining wall. It can be easier to wheel the bikes along the top. On reaching Rydal Mount, Wordsworth's final home until his death in 1850, go down the steep drive to the main road, turn left towards Ambleside and then right in a quarter of a mile or so over Pelter Bridge and follow the Under Loughrigg road back to the starting point.

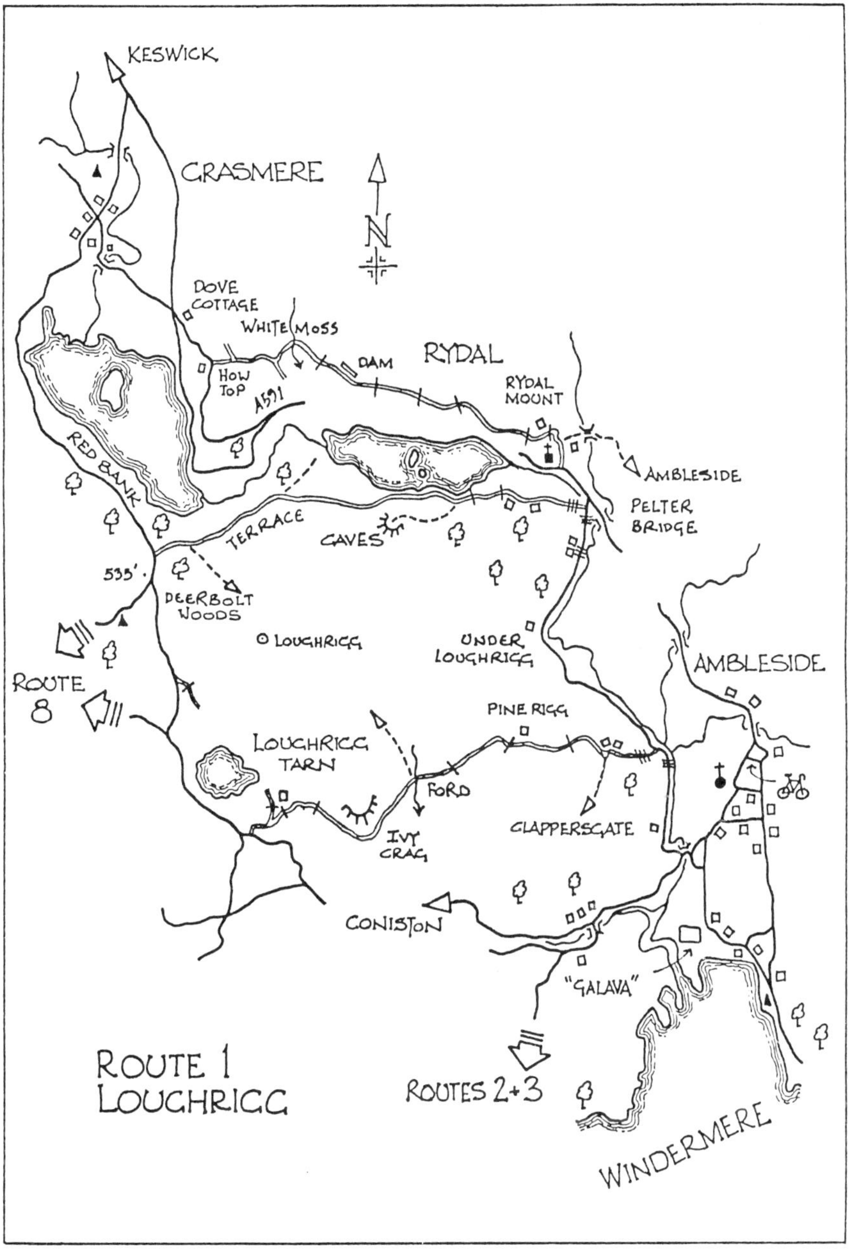
KESWICK
GRASMERE
N
DOVE COTTAGE
WHITE MOSS
RYDAL
DAM
HOW TOP
A591
RYDAL MOUNT
RED BANK
AMBLESIDE
PELTER BRIDGE
TERRACE
CAVES
535'.
DEERBOLT WOODS
LOUGHRIGG
UNDER LOUGHRIGG
AMBLESIDE
ROUTE 8
PINE RIGG
LOUGHRIGG TARN
FORD
IVY CRAG
CLAPPERSGATE
CONISTON
"GALAVA"
ROUTE 1
LOUGHRIGG
ROUTES 2+3
WINDERMERE

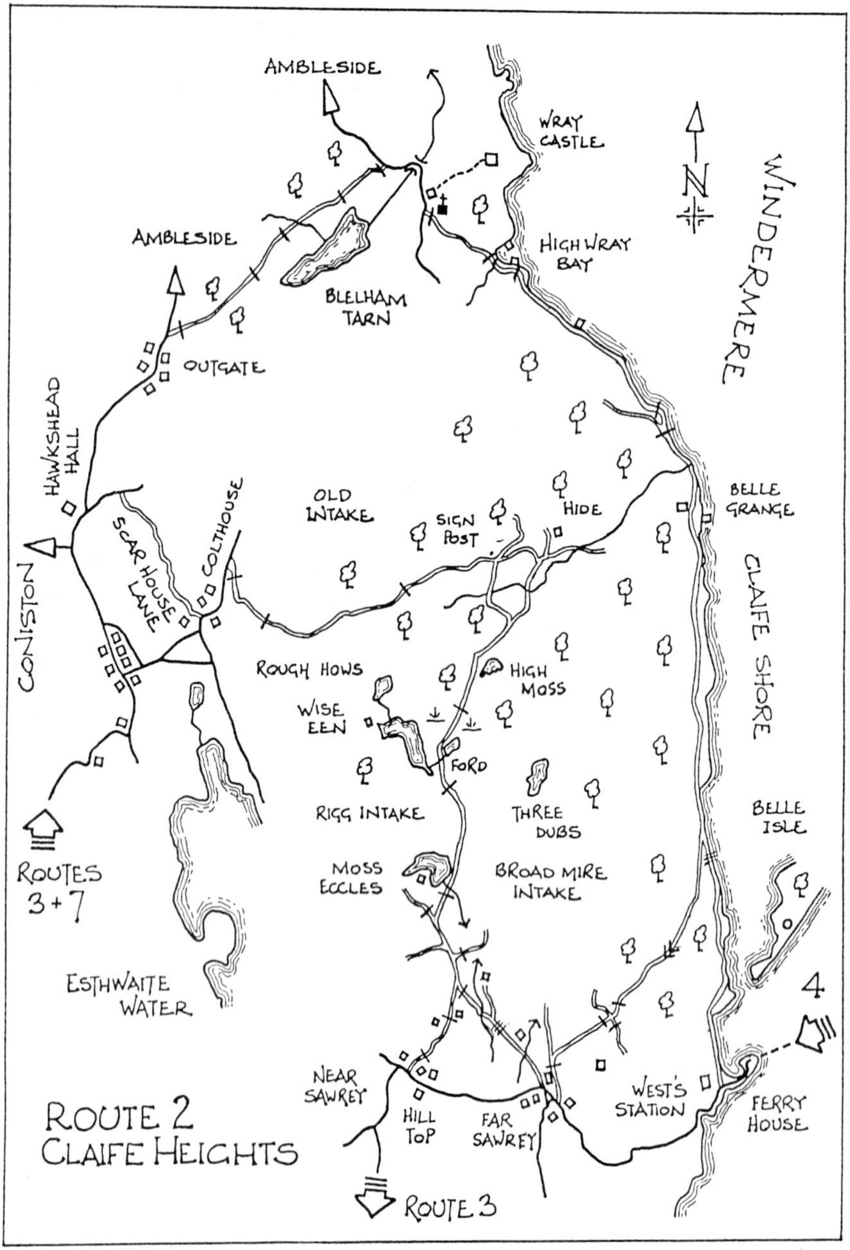
AMBLESIDE
WRAY CASTLE
N
WINDERMERE
AMBLESIDE
HIGH WRAY BAY
BLELHAM TARN
OUTGATE
HAWKSHEAD HALL
OLD INTAKE
SIGN POST
HIDE
BELLE GRANGE
CONISTON
SCAR HOUSE LANE
COLTHOUSE
CLAIFE SHORE
ROUGH HOWS
HIGH MOSS
WISE EEN
FORD
RIGG INTAKE
THREE DUBS
BELLE ISLE
ROUTES 3+7
MOSS ECCLES
BROAD MIRE INTAKE
ESTHWAITE WATER
4
NEAR SAWREY
WEST'S STATION
FERRY HOUSE
HILL TOP
FAR SAWREY
ROUTE 2
CLAIFE HEIGHTS
ROUTE 3

2 Claife Heights

TO APPROACH Route 2 from Ambleside follow the A593 Coniston Road as far as Clappersgate and then dip down to the left over Brathay Bridge on the road to Hawkshead. Having visited the Roman Fort of "Galava" (Waterhead) whilst in Ambleside it is interesting to think that this stretch of road alongside the river is probably one of the Lake District's first roads. Roman Legions under Hadrian, marching towards Hardknott and Ravenglass, came this way south of the river as far as Little Langdale, the journey with them, however, is short as they follow the river bank towards Skelwith Bridge whereas Route 2 takes the main road to the left — Route 9 catches up with them later though. Cycle on around Pull Wyke Bay until a turning on the left, signposted Wray Castle, is reached. Half a mile along here just before the church is the gatehouse to the "Castle".

Wray Castle was built in 1840 as a Gothic fantasy and is worth a look if only to see what strange ideas the idle rich of 150 years ago had when it came to retirement homes! Dropping down behind the church to the twin boathouses on High Wray Bay, a well maintained track leads all the way to the Bowness Ferry, the only habitation on the way being Belle Grange at the half way point. Here, at Belle Grange, there used to be another Windermere Ferry to Low Millerground on the opposite shore linking the two important Market Towns of the day, Kendal and Hawkshead. The old bell that called the boatman from Belle Grange can still be seen in the gable end of a cottage at Low Millerground, built in 1612.

If of a nervous disposition it is wise not to visit this side of the lake after dark for fear of bumping into the "Crier of Claife". It is said that one misty night a ghostly voice called the boatman over and when the poor bloke was seen again, several days later, he was out of his mind. He died a couple of days later never having recovered from his ordeal. The spirit was banished to a quarry on the heights but still on misty moonlight nights a wheezing hooded figure calls "Boat" . . .

Just before the cattle grid, where the wooded track becomes a surfaced road, a steep bridleway is signposted to the right. It is *very* steep but eventually after a bit of pushing it comes out from the trees to become a walled lane that emerges behind the inn in Far Sawrey.

To arrive on Route 2 from Windermere, freewheel down the hill from the railway station to Bowness, cross the lake to Ferry House and struggle up the hill to the Sawrey Inn. A decision has to be made here, whether to patronise the inn (it should be about lunch time by now) or to further literary knowledge by visiting Beatrix Potter's cottage just up the road at Hill Top.

From both of the Sawreys, walled tracks lead to Claife Heights, meeting in half a mile or so. The "roads" over Claife were created in 1794 following acts of parliament to enclose the common land and therefore increase agricultural production. The lower enclosures on the valley floor are the inby land, heavily manured and used for intensive winter grazing whilst above about 500' larger areas of intake or rough pasture were drained and limed. These intakes still survive on Claife the route passing between Rigg and Broadmire and then on its way down towards Colthouse, Old and Rough Hows.

The numerous tarns that catch the sun — when it shines — are all artificial and were dammed at the turn of the century to provide much needed water power for the mills in the valley. Three Dubs was built in 1908 as the date on the boathouse declares and here on Moss Eccles, Beatrix Potter used to row to relax.

Navigation on Claife is a bit dodgy at the best of times especially since the intervention of the forestry commission who create new roads faster than the ordnance survey can keep up with them. From the top of the rise after Moss Eccles, Wise Een can be seen, really two tarns with the track running between them through a deep muddy ford. To enjoy this at its best it must be taken at speed, the two resulting plumes of dirty water gracefully meeting high in the air and then promptly falling — on the person following. Once completely soaked, pedal up the grassy bank ahead, through a swamp and into the forest via a gate in the corner of the walls where a muddy track runs past High Moss to a turning circle at the start of a forest road. Follow this until a sweeping right hand bend climbs out to a cross roads and, observing the signpost pointing left to Hawkshead, continue uphill in this direction.

A gate leads to the top of an exceptionally wild descent of just over a mile to Colthouse. This is the continuation of the old pony route from Windermere via Belle Grange to Hawkshead that was mentioned earlier. Turn left at the bottom of the track and then right in Colthouse, by the village notice board, along Scar House Lane between lines of upended Brathay Flags, an unusual and local form of fencing. Turn left at the end of the lane and join the main Ambleside to Hawkshead road. Here, just to the left, are the remains of Hawkshead Hall, the grange or abbey farm belonging to Furness Abbey. From here the monks controlled the affairs of their estates as far afield as Grange in Borrowdale and Brotherilkeld in Upper Eskdale.

At Outgate, the village which grew around the gate leading from the enclosed lands to the common fell, bear right along a bridleway (signposted) alongside Blelham Tarn to rejoin the lane to Wray Castle, turn left for Ambleside.

To get back to Windermere, via the Bowness ferry, simply return to the beginning of the chapter and follow it back to Ferry House, the only difference being instead of turning right at the cattle grid to Far Sawrey continue alongside the lake. At the end of the track the ruinous archways on the left are all that remains of a summerhouse built on the site of "West's first station". In his book, "A guide to the lakes in Cumberland, Westmorland

Water Splash at Wise Een Tarn. *(Dave Lee)*

and Lancashire" published in 1778, Thomas West guides the visitor from station to station, for each one giving detailed romantic descriptions of the unfolding panoramas. Finally turn left and pass Ferry House, once a fine hotel, now the laboratories of the Freshwater Biological Association, to arrive back at the ferry to Bowness.

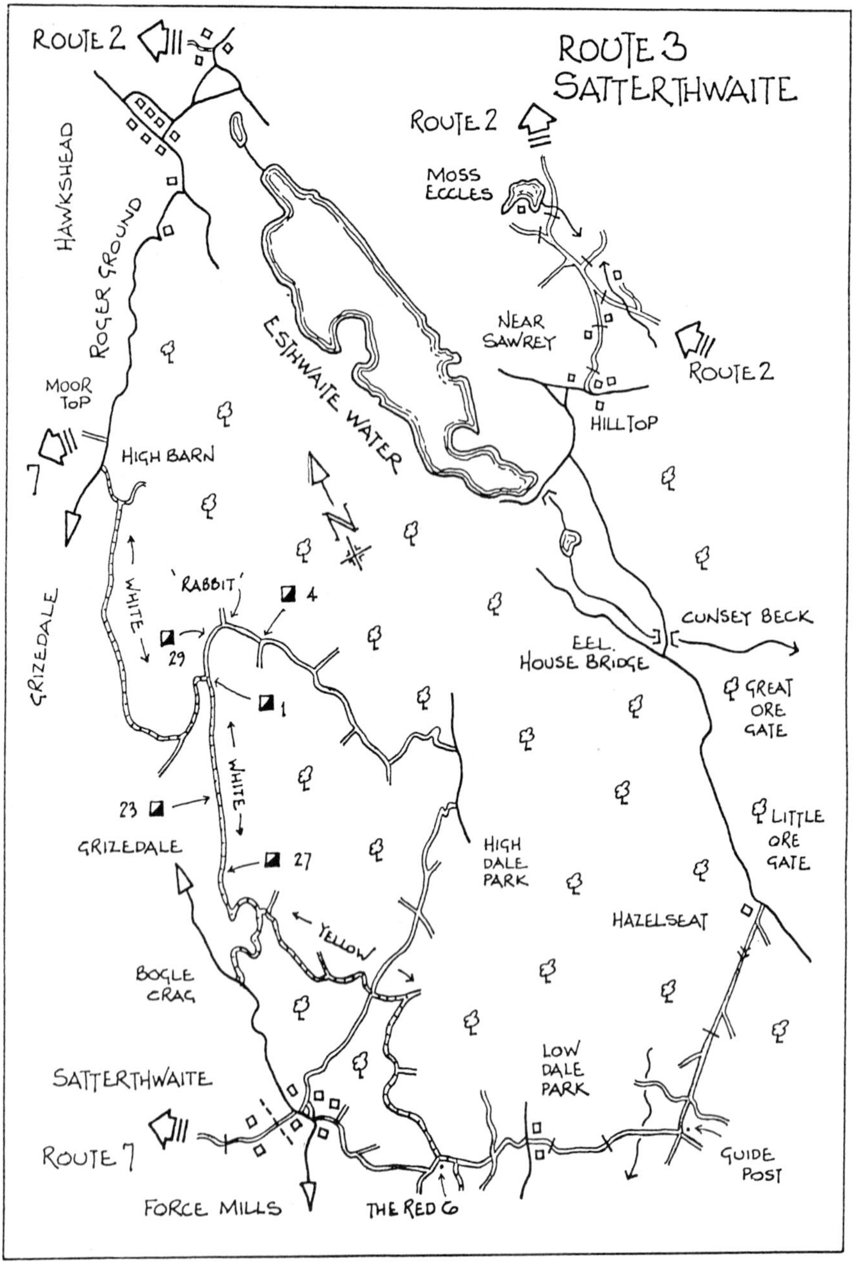
ROUTE 3
SATTERTHWAITE
ROUTE 2
ROUTE 2
MOSS ECCLES
NEAR SAWREY
ROUTE 2
HILLTOP
HAWKSHEAD
ROGER GROUND
ESTHWAITE WATER
MOOR TOP
HIGH BARN
7
N
'RABBIT'
4
29
1
WHITE
WHITE
GRIZEDALE
CUNSEY BECK
EEL HOUSE BRIDGE
GREAT ORE GATE
23
GRIZEDALE
27
HIGH DALE PARK
LITTLE ORE GATE
HAZELSEAT
YELLOW
BOGLE CRAG
LOW DALE PARK
SATTERTHWAITE
ROUTE 7
GUIDE POST
FORCE MILLS
THE RED 6

3 Satterthwaite

THIS IS an extension to Route 2 that replaces 4 miles of easy going bridleway with a 10 mile route not recommended for the faint hearted.

From Beatrix Potter's house at Hill Top, Near Sawrey take the first left and then fork left. A little way down the road is an unusual traffic sign, a red warning triangle not with a cow or even a deer but a *frog*. Be warned! Just before the main road is reached, Cunsey Beck, the outflow from Esthwaite Water, is crossed at Eel House Bridge. Stopping about here and thinking of the sheer power of the water is just what the engineers of the Backbarrow and Cunsey Furnace Company must have done in 1710 for it was half a mile further downstream that they sited one of the largest blast furnaces of the age. The beck was diverted via a headrace to power the bellows and the surrounding woodlands were felled to provide charcoal. Even now, over 275 years later, two stands of oak to the right of the road are known as Great and Little Ore Gate.

At Hazel Seat pass through the timber yard and a steep track running south-west climbs, slipping and sliding up and over, to drop with alarming suddenness towards a new forest road not yet marked on the OS maps. It is in fact so steep in places that a rear pannier rack really comes in handy — to sit on to avoid going over the handlebars. Crossing directly over the road the way continues for another 150 yards in the same direction before reaching a signposted crossroads and turning right towards Low Dale Park.

On closing the first gate, the right of way as marked on the 1:25000 OS maps cuts up the hill to the wall on the right and then follows it seemingly cross country to the farm. After getting to the buildings, bear right through the farmyard and then left just before the last barn to reach the road at the bottom, watching out for the traffic.

Through the picnic area there is a ford for the reckless and a footbridge for the more cautious, both of which lead up a path that thinks it's a stream for 50 yards before branching left through a gap in the fence. Probably pushing up to cross one forest road and then still pushing to the next casts a doubt into the mind, "Why did I spend £400 on a bike to push it through a forest?". The answer of course is clear because if the road is followed right for a bit and the left fork is taken at the red number 6 a turning circle is reached. From here, heading right is the sort of fast and furious descent that restores the confidence, remembering what goes up must come down.

At Satterthwaite church go right, right and right between the cottages and at the top of the hill is Breasty Haw. The way through to High Dale Park can be divided into three sections, the first two well graded and marked by blue topped posts, the third being rough, unmarked and with a very bumpy last drop to the road. Between the first and second sections there is a chance to

A Forestry Commission cycle route. *(Mike Hyde)*

retire by turning left and following the yellow cycle route to Bogle Crag and then the white to High Barn. Back at High Dale Park follow the flat road left for a couple of minutes and then it all has to be done again — this time even worse than the last, only shorter. Soon coming to a forest road turn right and right again, still on good surfaces, until suddenly the end of the line is reached. More mud, more trimmings and fallen trees and more swearing either at the Forestry Commission or the author and at last arrival at an escape route. Yet another forest road, this one leading past a large wooden rabbit to sanity and the white bicycle route to High Barn. The orienteering controls are a good way of keeping check on the route, go right at 4, straight on at 29 and right again at 1. Now follow the white bikes home, at least to the top of Roger Ground.

4 Troutbeck

ALTHOUGH IT may not look like it, Route 4 is a circular route. It can be started either at Ambleside or Windermere and its loose ends should be joined by following Route 2, backwards along the Claife shore.

From Ambleside, climb rapidly up behind the Ambleside and Langdale Mountain Rescue Headquarters to join the main east/west drovers' road across the Southern Lakes. Cattle would have been gathered in Eskdale from the farms along the more fertile west coast and then driven over the passes to Little Langdale and Ambleside (Route 8) then to Troutbeck (Route 4), Kentmere (Route 5) and Sadgill (Route 6). Finally, at Sadgill, a choice of two routes one north via Gatesgarth Pass and Swindale to Shap and the other south along Longsleddale to join the main north/south drove road at Lambrigg Park near Sedbergh. The roads themselves tended to be very distinctive, being both wide and level. Notice how from High Skelghyll this particular section contours around the slopes of Wansfell, whereas a more direct packhorse trail may have zigzagged over it. Lastly, they kept to the fell sides above the inhabited land in the valley bottoms, probably thinking of the damage 500 head of prime beef stock would have caused in some yeoman farmer's back garden.

After the drive to Broad Ings is passed, enter the National Trust's Skelghyll Woods and ascend via series of hairpins to Jenkins Crag, a fine viewpoint overlooking Windermere towards the Langdale Pikes and Coniston Fells. This section of "Green Lane" has been attributed originally to the Romans making their way from the southern end of High Street to the fort of Galava at Waterhead, a hard walk by today's standards, without wearing a suit of armour!

At the cattle grid below High Skelghyll Farm, bear left through the little gate and up the hill to join the curiously named Hundreds Road. Towards the close of the seventeenth century the village of Troutbeck was really three smaller hamlets or hundreds, upper, middle and lower and each had its corresponding area of pasture on the hillside. Livestock were turned out each spring through the Longmire 'yeats' or gates and driven along either Nanny Lane or the Hundreds Road to their pasture to remain until winter. Shortly after joining the hundreds road, a stile on the left gives access to a stone pillar on the hillside. This is a Victorian viewing 'station' similar to those in Thomas West's book mentioned previously in Route 2. The Hundreds Road becomes Robin Lane and arrives in Troutbeck by the Post Office and Institute.

The village has changed little since the yeoman farmers of the 1600's built their houses along the road between Town End and Town Head, the only evidence of the twentieth century on the landscape being Limefitt Park, the

Camping and Caravan Site through which the route passes. Enter the site through the main gate, go along avenue 9 and behind the quaintly named Haybarns Inn to find a green metal gate leading to the fellside.

After climbing for 200 yards, join the larger track coming from the north and double back along this to the right. This is thought to be the continuation of the Roman Road over High Street running south to meet the main Kendal/Ambleside road in the vicinity of the hill fort on Allen Knott. At the gate leave the Romans to plod along Longmire Road and double back a second time to the start of the Garburn Road. Now depending on a) the time and b) the amount of energy remaining, a decision has to be made. Either the Garburn Pass, one of the roughest climbs in the area but giving the greatest satisfaction or the Dubbs Road to Windermere. Route 5 goes over the pass to Kentmere. However, a compromise can be made by climbing to the top of the pass and then turning round, holding on tight and flying back down to the Dubbs.

Once on the tarmac at the end of the walled lane, it's back with those Romans again. If High Street is extended south to the hill fort on Allen Knott and then joined to Kendal with a straight line it follows this lane exactly as far as Ings where it joins the main road. If this line is again extended this time in the opposite direction, it heads for Ambleside connecting with the earlier part of this route below the viewing Station.

A quick left, then right to coast down through the Common brings the route to the main A591 at Alice Howe. The start of the bridleway to Cleabarrow is through the unmarked gate 100 yards to the right. Now more by luck than judgement the route manages to miss out most of Windermere and Bowness but they can't be passed by without a brief word. Bowness is the older of the two, being situated on the narrowest part of the lake and hence the ideal place for a ferry between the two important markets of Kendal and Hawkshead.

Windermere, on the other hand, is totally a creation of the railway age. Until the trains came in 1847 the hamlet of Birthwaite lived a relatively quiet existence up on the fellside overlooking the lake. Not all of it is Victorian though as the way passes through the Droomer housing estate. Take care on crossing the railway line, even though there are only 15 trains a day, and emerge between numbers 30 and 32 Ghyll Road. Now follow the pavement round and disappear down the tarmac bridleway behind the houses. Where the path turns sharp right to High Lickbarrow go through the gate and the track ahead leads to the Crook road opposite the Windermere Golf Club House. From the track junction half a mile back, this route coincides with the last stages of the "Dales Way", an eighty mile walk from Ilkley to Bowness described in the Dalesman Book by Colin Speakman. Turn right at the clubhouse and descend to the ferry at Bowness, cross to the other side and follow Route 2, in reverse along the Claife shore back to Ambleside.

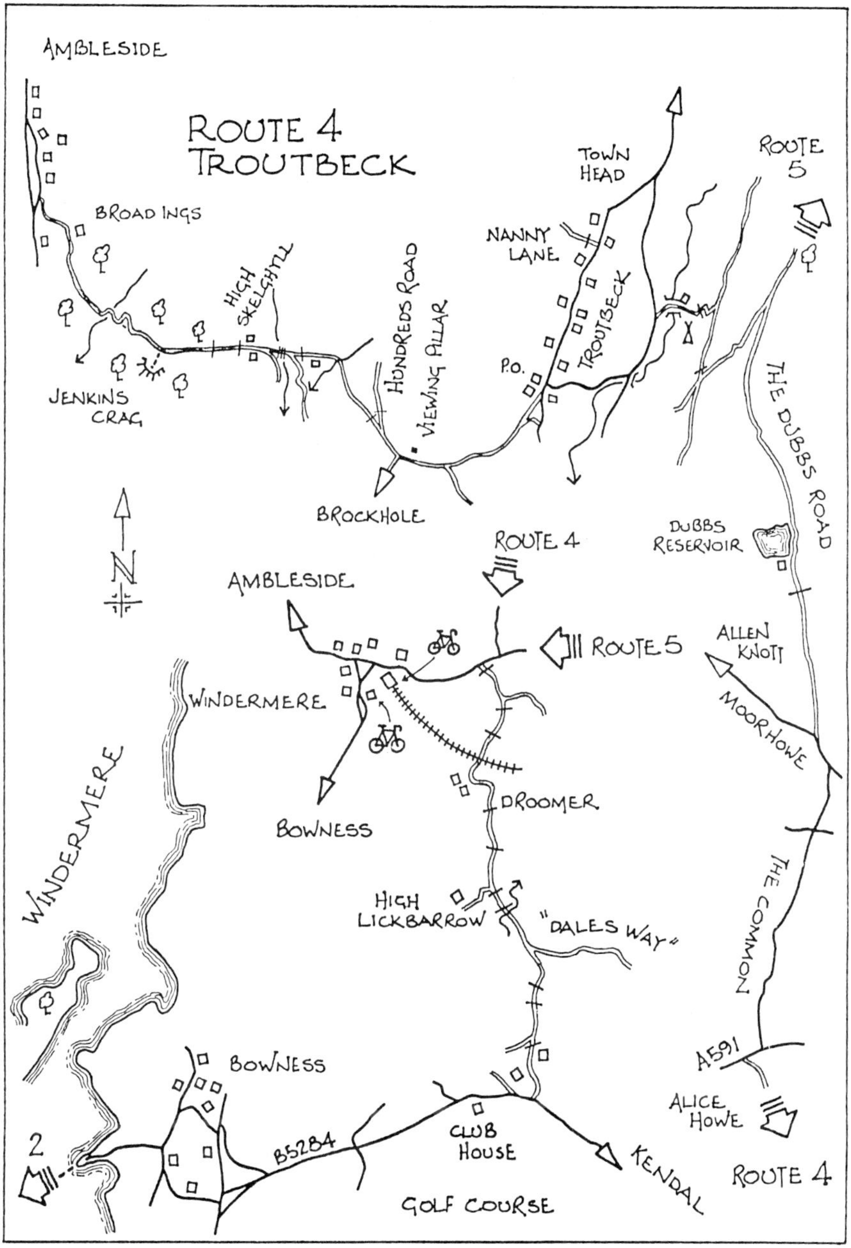
ROUTE 4
TROUTBECK
AMBLESIDE
BROAD INGS
JENKINS CRAG
HIGH SKELGHYLL
HUNDREDS ROAD
VIEWING PILLAR
BROCKHOLE
TOWN HEAD
NANNY LANE
TROUTBECK
P.O.
ROUTE 5
THE DUBBS ROAD
DUBBS RESERVOIR
ROUTE 4
AMBLESIDE
ROUTE 5
ALLEN KNOTT
MOORHOWE
WINDERMERE
WINDERMERE
BOWNESS
DROOMER
HIGH LICKBARROW
"DALES WAY"
THE COMMON
A591
ALICE HOWE
BOWNESS
2
B5284
CLUB HOUSE
KENDAL
ROUTE 4
GOLF COURSE

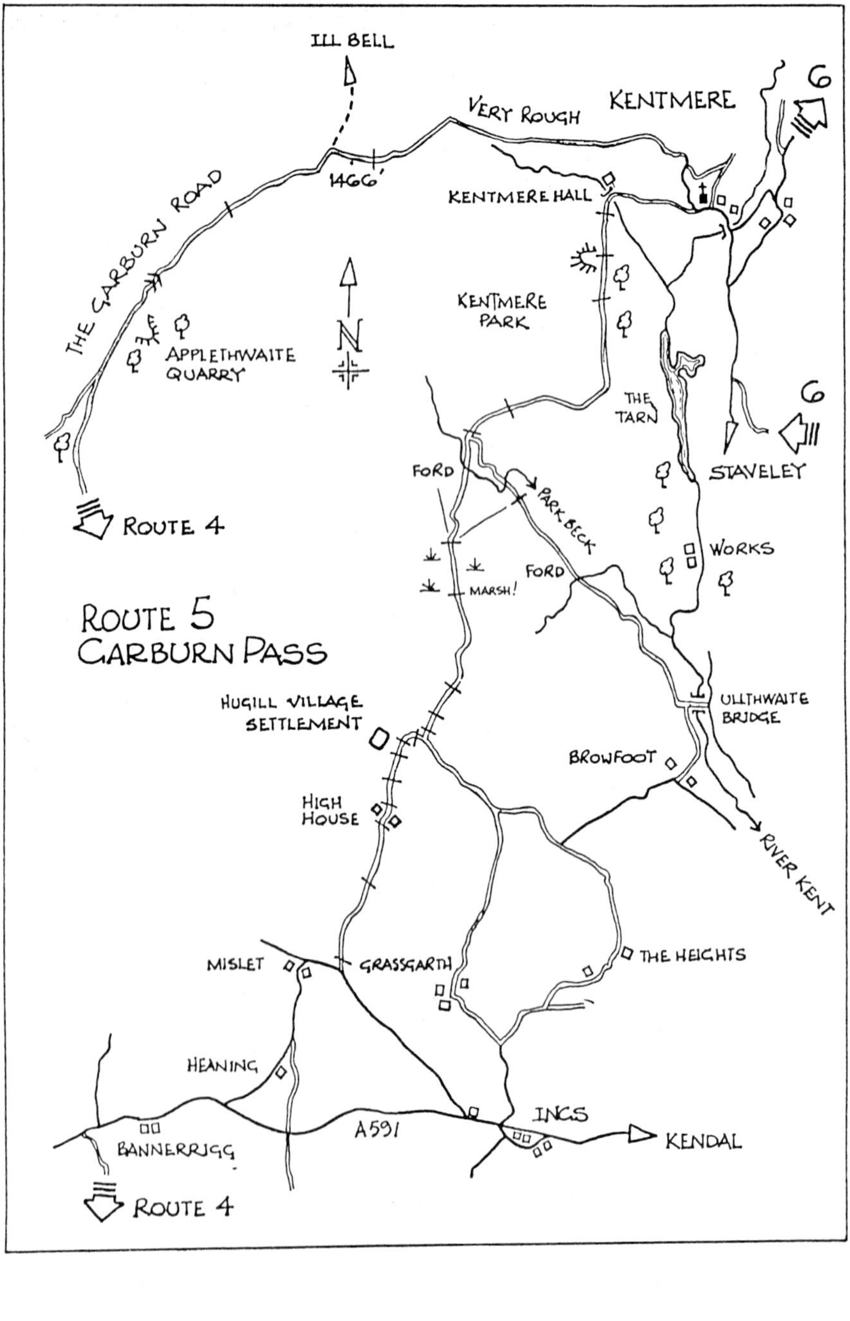

ILL BELL
VERY ROUGH
KENTMERE
6
1466
KENTMERE HALL
THE GARBURN ROAD
KENTMERE PARK
APPLETHWAITE QUARRY
N
THE TARN
6
STAVELEY
FORD
PARK BECK
ROUTE 4
WORKS
FORD
MARSH!
ROUTE 5
GARBURN PASS
HUGILL VILLAGE SETTLEMENT
ULLTHWAITE BRIDGE
BROWFOOT
HIGH HOUSE
RIVER KENT
MISLET
GRASSGARTH
THE HEIGHTS
HEANING
INGS
BANNERRIGG
A591
KENDAL
ROUTE 4

5   The Garburn Pass

BY NO STRETCH of the imagination is this a "Circular route based on Ambleside, Coniston or Keswick" but is in fact an interesting extension to Route 4 for those with large amounts of surplus energy. As already mentioned, the Garburn Road was a vital link in the pre-turnpike drove road across the southern lakes and considering this it is strange that it has always been so rough. In a survey of roads in the area made by the High Constable of Kendal in 1730 it was described as being "Not passable for either man or horse to travel without danger of being bogged in moss or lamed among the stones". The lower section as far as Applethwaite Quarry is still reasonably surfaced but after that little has changed and the rough going makes this one of the most technically demanding climbs in the book.

If the way up was bad then just take a look over the other side — a mile of pure endurance test bumping its way down to Kentmere. Don't be afraid to get off and walk in places, it's less risky! The river Kent passes through the centre of the village and half a mile south flows into the remains of Kentmere Tarn. Once much larger but now almost totally silted up, it once provided a valuable source of Diatomaceous Earth (Diatoms are the remains of tiny water plants) which amongst other exciting things was made into heat insulating bricks and soundproof boarding.

At the church, double back on the track to Kentmere Hall where, at the end of the farm buildings, is a curious tower. This is a pele built in the 14th century as protection for the residents from the Scots raiders who, under Robert the Bruce, had the nasty habit of pouring over the Nan Bield Pass and ransacking the village on their way to Lancaster.

Bearing left at the Hall, the track heads steeply up the hillside above the trees towards another of the many local quarries and then follows the wall contouring around the slopes of Kentmere Park. At the gate above Park Beck, a faint track leads down to Ulthwaite Bridge and Staveley but this route follows the left hand bank for a hundred yards or so before crossing and then the continuation can be seen climbing through the heather towards a group of trees on the skyline. From there, two walls converge at a gate and a swamp! Follow the wall and after four more gates arrive at a junction, the well defined walled track to the left leads by either of two splendid routes to Ings but turning sharp right through yet another gate and along a grassy terrace, Route 5 arrives at Hugill Village Settlement. This is typical of the earliest British communities being situated high on the fellside above the inhabitable valley bottoms. Obviously none of the drystone hutments have survived the ravages of time but some of the entrances and walkways can still be spotted by the more observant.

If you do wish to visit the village, please leave the bikes against the wall

A misty afternoon – the top of the Garburn Pass.   (Mike Hyde)

and go by foot as the settlement is on private land and visitors are permitted only by the good nature of the landowner. Back in the saddle again, a good farm track leads down through High House Farm to the Main Road near Mislet.

Although this is now only a B road, and a quiet one at that, it was, before the Victorian creation of Windermere, a much more important route from Kendal to Ambleside. It may even, as mentioned in the previous chapter, have been planned by the Roman surveyors under Agricola. It is exactly here that a southerly continuation of High Street over Applethwaite Common would have met the direct line from Kendal to Waterhead via Jenkins Crag.

As stated at the beginning of this chapter, it is not a circle but an extension to Route 4 and, to get back on it again, turn right and first left to arrive on the main A591 just below Bannerigg.

6 Longsleddale

ADMITTEDLY, this is a bit out on a limb but for those who like a bit of solitude as they cycle this is the place to go. It is a fair old way in by main road either from Ambleside or Kendal and just to confuse matters even more the route description will start from Kentmere, for no other reason than that to my way of thinking the best way into these silent valleys is via the Garburn Pass (Route 5).

From Kentmere church, cross the river at Low Bridge and turn immediately left for Green Quarter. The Quarters must be to Kentmere what the Hundreds are to Troutbeck the only strange thing being that now there are only three, Green, Crag and Hallow Bank. Where is the fourth? It should be where Kentmere Park is now. Towards Hallow Bank, an unsurfaced road is signposted to Sadgill and this is what we want, a peaceful climb up past Stile End with only the cows to talk to and a crazy little descent to Sadgill.

Halfway down at the gate above Tills Hole it is worth stopping to reflect on the tranquil scene below. If planners had had their wicked way either British Rail's West Coast mainline to Glasgow or the M6 could have come this way between Kendal and Penrith.

On emerging from between the farm buildings to cross the river, imagine having to wait two days for the floods to subside, as travellers of old sometimes had to do until, in 1717, they petitioned successfully for a bridge.

Turn right along the road and right again in half a mile over the cattle grid on the drive to Tills Hole. If a cup of tea is needed by this time, then head left instead of right to Stockdale. From Tills, the bridleway to Garnett Bridge may just hold the record for the most gates to open and close, a total of 34 on a good day. The reason for this is that it's not really one track but a number of small ones linking together the many farms along this west side of the valley and because of this needs blow by blow instructions.

Go left immediately after crossing the river (again) then to the right of the spruce tree plantation to join the concrete drive from Toms Howe. This veers left over a cattle grid to join the road but carry straight on to Hill Cottage and Underhill Cottage (in ruins). At Well Foot pass uphill of the chicken shed and then the farmbuildings to drop down again through two gates to the driveway, this diversion is signposted well with blue arrows. At Hollin Foot, gate 8 if they are being counted, the upper fork leads to Wads Howe, where, to get through the farmyard, the route goes right through the gap in the wall being followed and then between the farm buildings to emerge the other side on a grassy terrace. At the next farm there is NO right of way through the buildings as seems obvious but it keeps above the wall on the right to pass through another gate, number 13, to enter a field usually

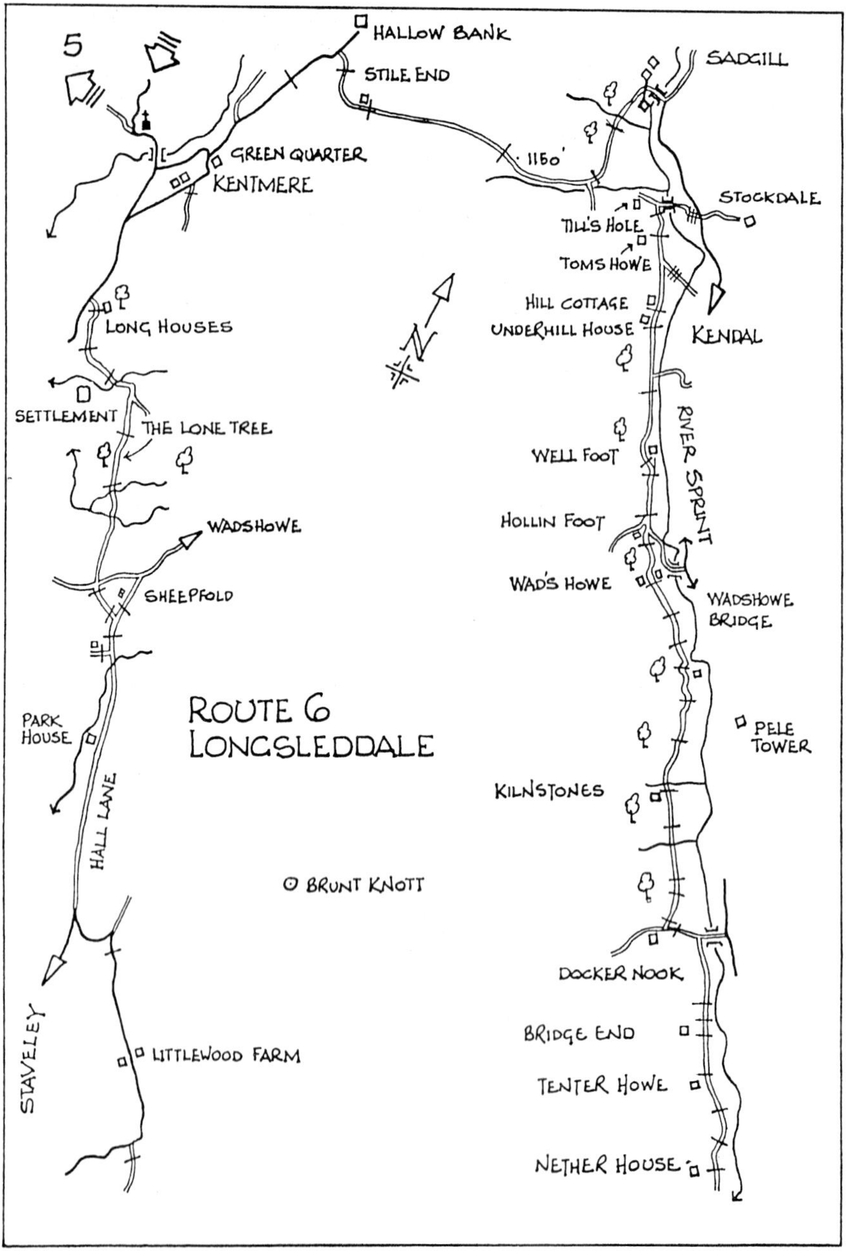
5
HALLOW BANK
STILE END
SADGILL
GREEN QUARTER
KENTMERE
1150'
STOCKDALE
TILL'S HOLE
TOMS HOWE
HILL COTTAGE
UNDERHILL HOUSE
KENDAL
LONG HOUSES
SETTLEMENT
THE LONE TREE
RIVER SPRINT
WELL FOOT
HOLLIN FOOT
WADSHOWE
WAD'S HOWE
SHEEPFOLD
WADSHOWE BRIDGE
ROUTE 6
LONGSLEDDALE
PARK HOUSE
PELE TOWER
KILNSTONES
HALL LANE
BRUNT KNOTT
DOCKER NOOK
STAVELEY
BRIDGE END
LITTLEWOOD FARM
TENTER HOWE
NETHER HOUSE

occupied by over-friendly horses. For a few sections here it becomes easier to follow, passes through the buildings at Kilnstones and keeps to the edge of the trees to join the drive to Docker Nook at a black gate with a white top. Head down the drive but turn right over the little bridge across Black Beck to enter a large grassy field.

On first assessment there appears to be no path but aim for the group of buildings dead ahead and when the river bank is touched a good track is joined. This leads to Bridge End, Tenter Howe and on towards Nether House Farm, being well signposted. Just after Nether House the track forks, the better surface going left across the river to join the road at Dale End and the rougher bit, naturally Route 6, going right alongside the wall, passing through it and climbing up to a signposted gate next to a prominent tree. Now a back wheel locked up slide diagonally right across the field just entered bringing the end in sight. Another new gate and fingerpost point the way along a lane towards Garnett Bridge. Don't drop down to the village though but go through another new gate, this one combined with a stile to enter a rough looking field. This bit is hard navigation but if the contour is roughly followed making use of the gateways in the walls a broad grassy track leads down to the Garnett Bridge Road at the LAST gate and a signpost with a different spelling of Sadgill (Sadghyll).

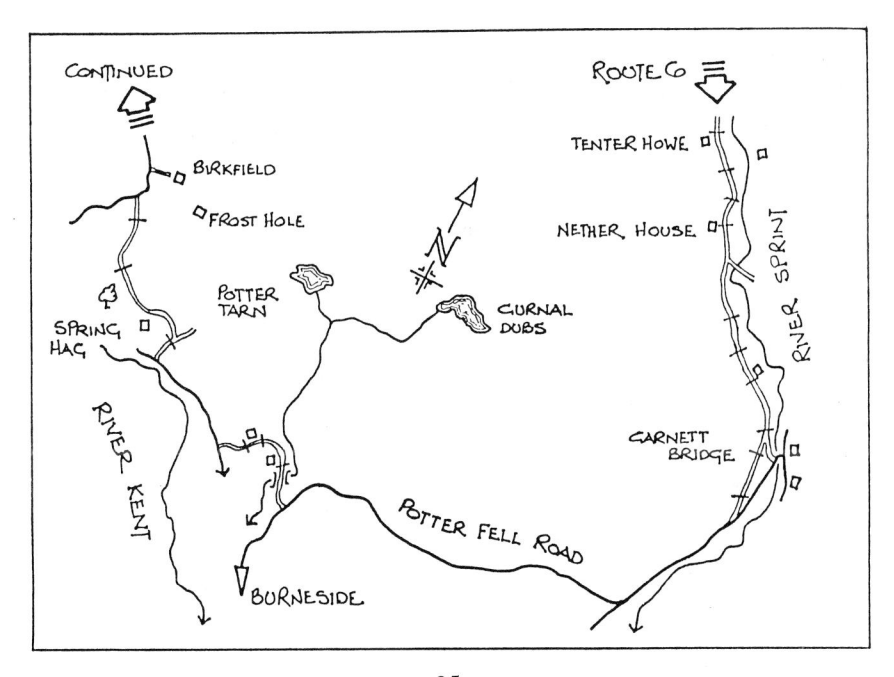

From above Garnett Bridge, a good view of the old mills can be had. Now turned into homes, they were in the last century part of the bobbin turning industry centred in this corner of the Lake District around Staveley. At the peak of the business during the period 1847–70, 49 mills were in production supplying roughly half of the British Textile Mills.

So there it is, the most intense set of directions in the whole book but necessary to avoid being shot at by irate farmers or trampled underfoot by unfriendly livestock. If it does all become too much, most of the farms have drives which lead to the main road and by heading right this can be followed round to gate 34.

A short section of bridleway from Mire Foot can be used to break the road journey and again in half a mile, by turning to the right to Spring Hag, another corner can be cut off. The beck that rushes down along Bridleway, part 1 is the combined outflow from Potter Tarn and Gurnall Dubbs, both dammed to provide extra water for Croppers, the large paper mill that can be seen down below in Burneside. At the end of Bridleway, part 2 turn right along the unfenced lane, past Littlewood Farm to meet Hall Lane, this in turn leads to Park House, home of Pony Trekking, and from here the bridleways are rejoined. After the first gate but before the complex sheep fold go left through a gate and cross diagonally right across the gently rising field to another gate. From this one begin descending, fording two small streams. After yet another gate, climb up towards a lone tree on the skyline. Now for the last bit, aim for the gate in the field corner and an exceptionally good lane winds down to the Kentmere valley at Long Houses.

7 Grizedale Forest

PART of Grizedale Forest has already been explored on Route 3 but to the west of the Satterthwaite to Hawkshead road there lies acres more fun for the discerning Mountain Biker. A word of warning though, Grizedale is private property owned entirely by the Forestry Commission and nobody has the right to cycle anywhere other than on definitive rights of way i.e. bridleways and as of 1988 on the specially waymarked forest bicycle routes. There are four colour coded routes as follows: White from High Barn to Bogle Crag and Yellow from Bogle Crag to Force Mills (both shown on Route 3) and then Red from Hawkshead Hill to Moor Top and Blue from Moor Top to Grizedale (Route 7). Details of these can be obtained from the Forestry Commission Centre at Grizedale (GR 335944).

Route 7 can be approached from either Coniston along the Hawkshead road, B5285 to High Cross and then along the Red cycle way to Moor Top or from Ambleside and Hawkshead by way of Roger Ground. Just through the gate at Moor Top the Red and Blue cycle ways diverge, follow Blue left past Juniper Tarn to the bridge over Grizedale Beck and here leave it as it descends to the left and climb straight ahead on the rougher bridleway. The area where the gradient eases is marked on OS maps as Grizedale Moor, not very moor-like but a fair indication of times past. In these harsh upland areas, timber has always been a viable crop whether it be for charcoal or pit props, bobbins or barrels and due to this demand these areas have been clear felled on more than one occasion, hence the legacy Hawkshead, Grizedale and Monk Coniston Moors.

The forest road along which the bridleway runs continues dead straight now for over a mile until, above Lawson Park, it bends to the left and a very muddy track to be followed goes straight ahead. At first the way passes between two areas of clear felling and re-seeding protected by ten foot high deer fences but in time an area of major devastation is reached. Bulldozer tracks and discarded brash make cycling impossible and it is with relief that the gate that leads to the open fellside is reached. The route is now indistinct and a number of narrow paths all lead in roughly the same direction. Keeping parallel to the lake all the paths eventually reach a wall running from left to right which can be followed, to the left to a gate. If a fence, not a wall, is encountered turn right not left.

After the exertions of Grizedale a rest at Parkamoor is well justified, the view across the lake to the Old Man and Wetherlam cannot be hurried. The farm, believed to be one of the oldest in the Lake District and acquired by the National Trust in 1968 is just above the site of one of the monastic bloomeries of the 15th century. Timber again was the main factor when it came to the siting of these bloomeries. It was a lot easier to carry 60

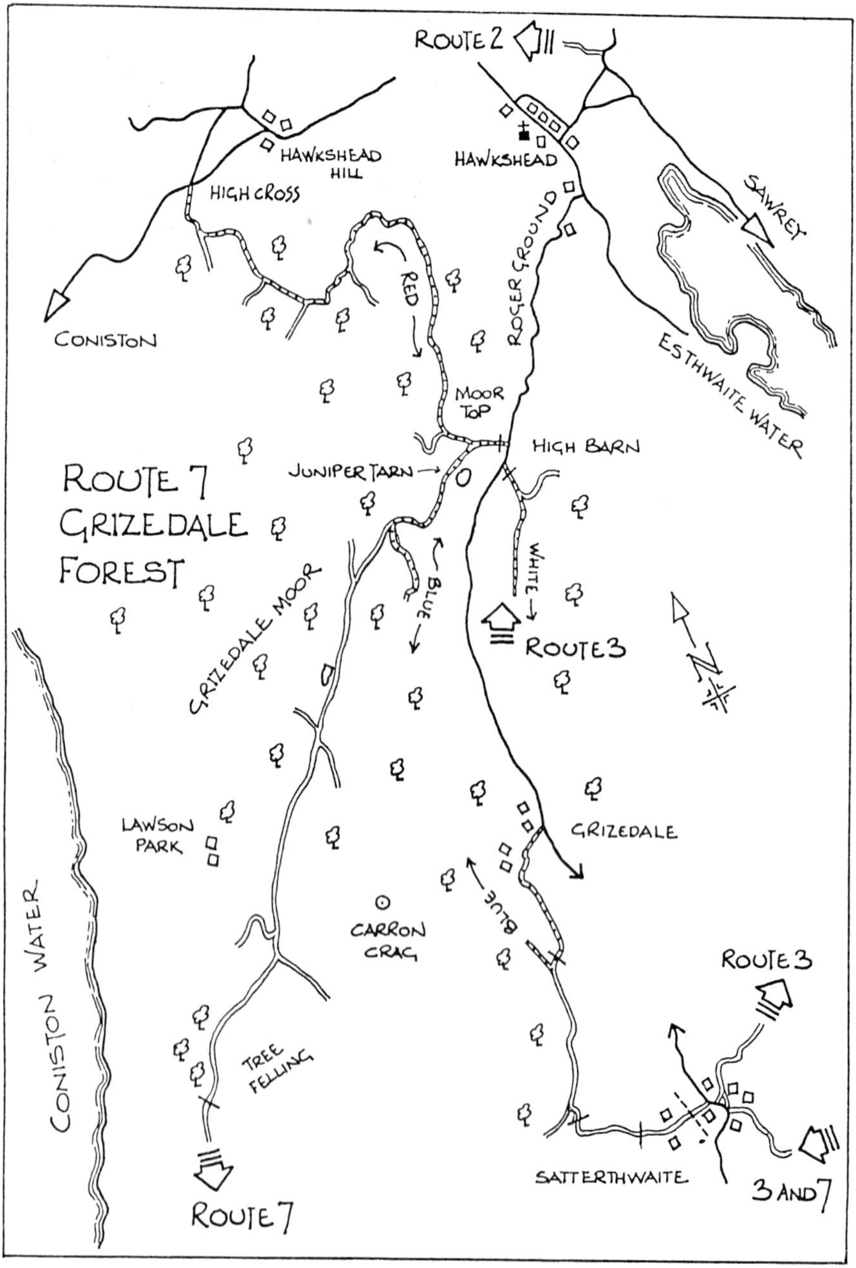
ROUTE 2
HAWKSHEAD HILL
HAWKSHEAD
HIGH CROSS
SAWREY
ROGER GROUND
RED
CONISTON
ESTHWAITE WATER
MOOR TOP
HIGH BARN
JUNIPER TARN
ROUTE 7
GRIZEDALE
FOREST
WHITE
BLUE
GRIZEDALE MOOR
ROUTE 3
N
LAWSON PARK
GRIZEDALE
CARRON CRAG
CONISTON WATER
ROUTE 3
TREE FELLING
SATTERTHWAITE
3 AND 7
ROUTE 7

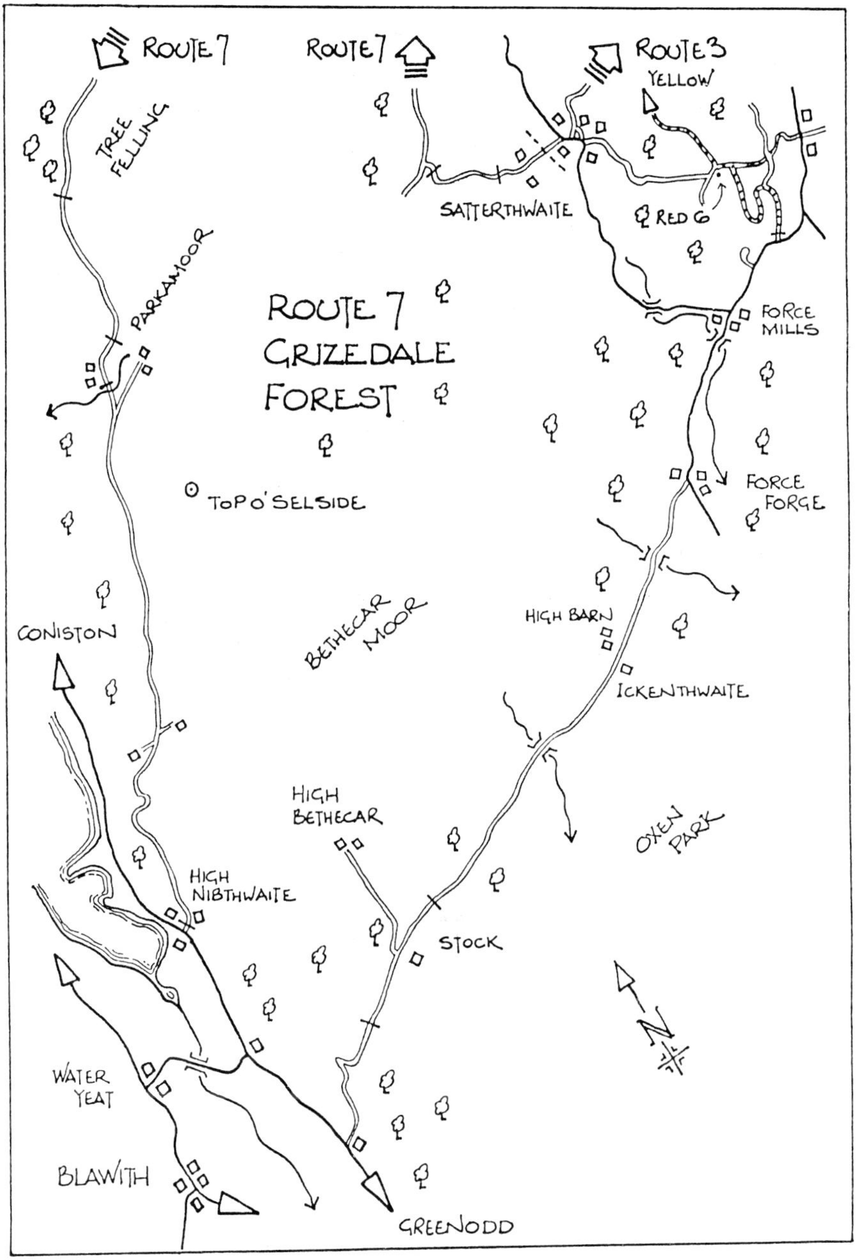
ROUTE 7
ROUTE 7
ROUTE 3
YELLOW
TREE FELLING
SATTERTHWAITE
RED 6
PARKAMOOR
ROUTE 7
GRIZEDALE
FOREST
FORCE MILLS
TOP O' SELSIDE
FORCE FORGE
BETHECAR MOOR
HIGH BARN
CONISTON
ICKENTHWAITE
HIGH BETHECAR
OXEN PARK
HIGH NIBTHWAITE
STOCK
N
WATER YEAT
BLAWITH
GREENODD

packhorse loads of ore to Parkamoor than to carry 30 acres of timber to Furness! The colliers who produced the necessary charcoal lived in semi-permanent wattle and daub hutments in the woods below and tended many dozen "steads" each.

Once revitalised, leave Parkamoor through the farmyard and cross the beck to join a superb track that runs all the way to Nibthwaite at the far end of the lake. Here, above Coniston Water, is without a doubt looking down on Swallows and Amazons country. Arthur Ransome's classic tales, more popular now than ever, have their roots deep in the heart of the Lake District. The Lake — it was always known just as "The Lake" — is mainly Windermere but surrounded by Coniston's fells, The Old Man for instance becomes Kanchenjunga, the Gondola is Captain Flint's Houseboat and the North Pole ("Winter Holiday" 1933) is somewhere in the vicinity of Waterhead, Ambleside!

From Nibthwaite there is a long road section that unfortunately is unavoidable when it comes to contriving circular routes. Head south towards Lowick Bridge but turn left in Blawith, pronounced Blaath, up the hill to Ickenthwaite and down the other side to Force Forge. Here, as the name suggests, there was a forge, in fact three dating from 1537, the sites of which were built over by two bobbin mills, hence further up the road Force Mills. At the mills turn right, go past the Blind Lane car park and enter the haven of the forest at the start of the Yellow Bicycle Route. This should be followed to the big red 6 mentioned in Route 3 where going to the left and then right in the turning circle is the start of the confidence restoring descent to Satterthwaite.

One thing that can bring a whole new concept to exploring the Lakes, or anywhere else for that matter, is an understanding of the meaning behind the place names. Take Satterthwaite for example, of Norse origin, the summer pasture in the clearing (saeter is the pasture and thveit is the clearing). Similarly Hawkshead and Ambleside when broken down become Houkrs and Hamels saeters. Once started this can go on ad nauseam, Griss is pigs so Grizedale becomes the pigs' valley, Dalr, fjall, gil, bekkr, tjörn — the list is endless and of course as well as the Vikings there were Romans, Anglo Saxons and Normans.

From the village those who have the energy can head for Breasty Haw by turning to Route 3, the rest may leave by the children's playground — no playing on the slides unless under ten years of age — and follow the final stage of the Lombard RAC rally (backwards) to Grizedale and then climb to Roger Ground to follow Route 3 home. The old hall where the Forestry Commission buildings now stand, demolished in 1952, was during the Second World War a Prisoner of War camp for German officers. The only one to escape, Franz von Verra, was later killed on the Russian front.

8 The Langdales

THIS ROUTE is either a short circuit or can be combined with Route 9 at Tilberthwaite ford to make a longer figure of eight. It is ideally started from Elterwater or from Ambleside either along the main road or via Route 1. From Coniston it can be approached via the southern end of Route 9 (which

The Langdales from Oak Howe. *(Mike Hyde)*

can then be done in either direction to arrive at the ford).
Elterwater as a village evolved totally around the Huddlestons Gunpowder Works, opened in 1824 on the site of what is now the Langdale timeshare complex, the old valley road running alongside the river from Skelwith Bridge (now a footpath), through the centre of the village, through the Powder works and joining the present B5343 at Chapel Stile. Route 8 leaves the village over the bridge, past the Youth Hostel and forks right twice, once at the hotel and once at Elterwater Hall, signposted as a dead end to become the old quarry road to Spout Crag.
It was from local quarries such as this that most of the building materials for the houses, works and walls were obtained as well as providing high quality roofing slates for export. Bayesbrown, the farm between the two quarries, is among the oldest in the valley, being recorded during the reign of

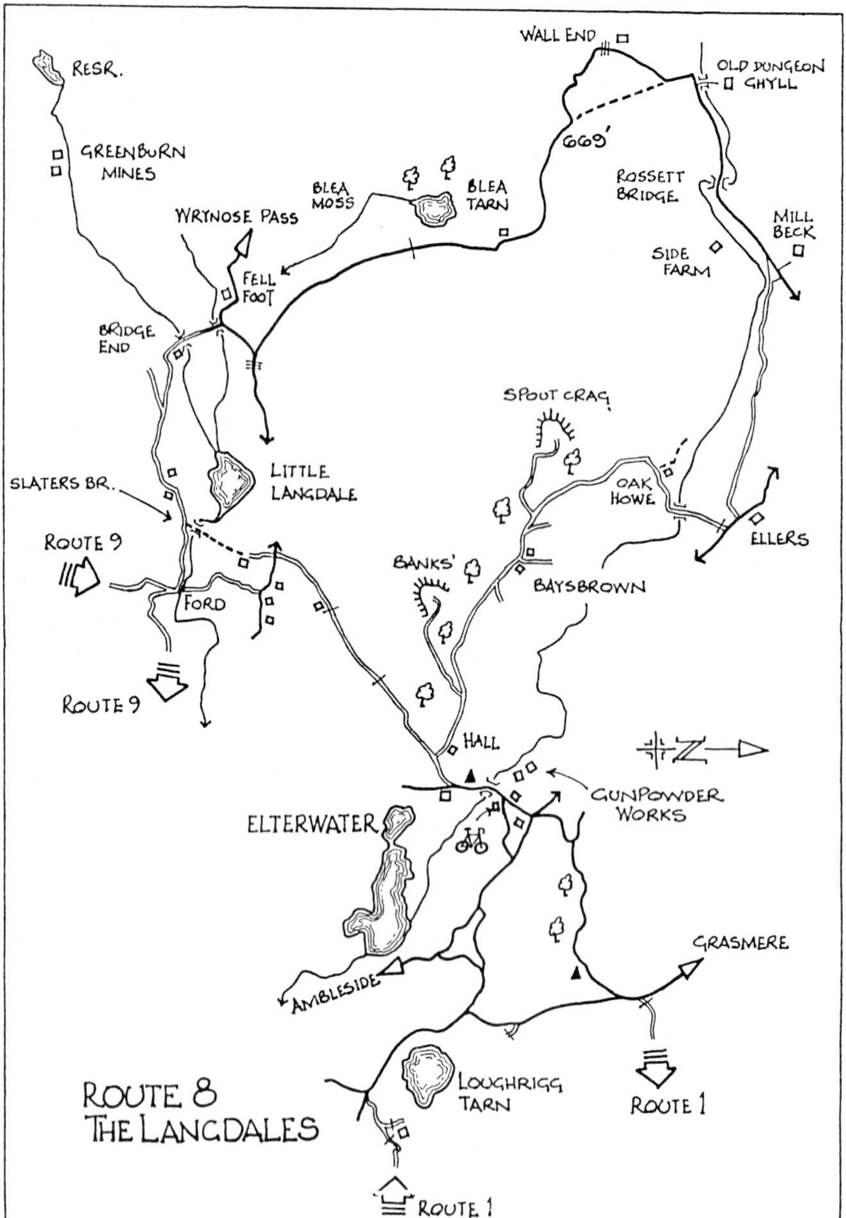
RESR.
GREENBURN MINES
WALL END
OLD DUNGEON GHYLL
669'
BLEA MOSS
BLEA TARN
ROSSETT BRIDGE
WRYNOSE PASS
MILL BECK
SIDE FARM
FELL FOOT
BRIDGE END
SPOUT CRAG
LITTLE LANGDALE
SLATERS BR.
OAK HOWE
ROUTE 9
ELLERS
BANKS'
BAYSBROWN
FORD
ROUTE 9
HALL
GUNPOWDER WORKS
ELTERWATER
GRASMERE
AMBLESIDE
LOUGHRIGG TARN
ROUTE 1
ROUTE 8
THE LANGDALES
ROUTE 1

Elizabeth I when it was purchased by the Braithwaites of Ambleside Hall. Pass between the farm buildings and follow the continuation of the track to Oak Howe. Most of the farms lining the valley, Bayesbrown, Oak Howe, Ellers, Mill Beck and Side Farm appear on the first accurate map of Great Langdale drawn in 1770 by Thomas Jefferys in response to the Royal Society of Arts offering a prize of £100 for new county maps produced at a scale of at least one inch to the mile.

Leave Oak Howe to the right of the buildings and cross the river on the new footbridge built by the Friends of the Lake District, touch the main road for a mere 100 yards and turn left along the "old valley road" as shown on Jefferys' map, to the New Dungeon Ghyll Hotel. As the river is crossed again the old Rossett Bridge can be used for posterity and almost all of the old road has now been travelled. Almost all because from the Old Dungeon Ghyll, a farm converted to a Packhorse Inn, the final section to Blea Tarn followed the wall straight up. Luckily, it is now only a footpath and the road assumes easier gradients, still 1:4 via Wall End Farm.

Look back across Great Langdale at the hump of Pike o'Stickle with its twin screes falling to the valley floor, there in 1947 were discovered some of the earliest traces of man in central Lake District. A neolithic axe factory, in use around 2700 BC where axes were roughed out prior to being transported, maybe on the oldest of tracks across Sty Head to the settlements on the coast there to be polished and exported as far afield as Ireland and maybe even Poland. Back to the route though, hurtling down to Little Langdale can be an interesting experience but don't forget to slow down enough to try and spot the small terraced mound behind Fell Foot Farm. This is thought to be a "Thingmount" or assembly place where Viking leaders from all parts of the Lake District held their meetings or "things". There may even have been a summer shelter or "shieling" at Blea Moss above us on the other side of the beck. Turn right at the road junction towards Wrynose Pass and left along the track to Bridge End crossing both the Brathay and Greenburn Beck before bearing left above the tarn towards the Slater Bridge.

The large track met joining from above right is the old mine road from the Greenburn Mines. The workings were commenced in about 1805 and five veins, Long Crag, Pave York, Gossan, Sump and Low Gill yielded quite large amounts of both Copper Pyrites and Copper Oxide. Over the wall to the left is the famous "Slaters Bridge" named after the quarry men. It spans the Brathay in two stages, the first humped in the true packhorse style and the second a clapper bridge of slate flags. Three hundred yards further on is the ford which marks the intersection of Routes 8 and 9.

To return to Elterwater, ford the river, a good effort if it can be done without getting the boots wet, and climb up the lane to Little Langdale chapel. Turn left along the road until, opposite the drive to High Birk Howe, the continuation of the packhorse route over the slaters' bridge from Tilberthwaite leads back to the village.

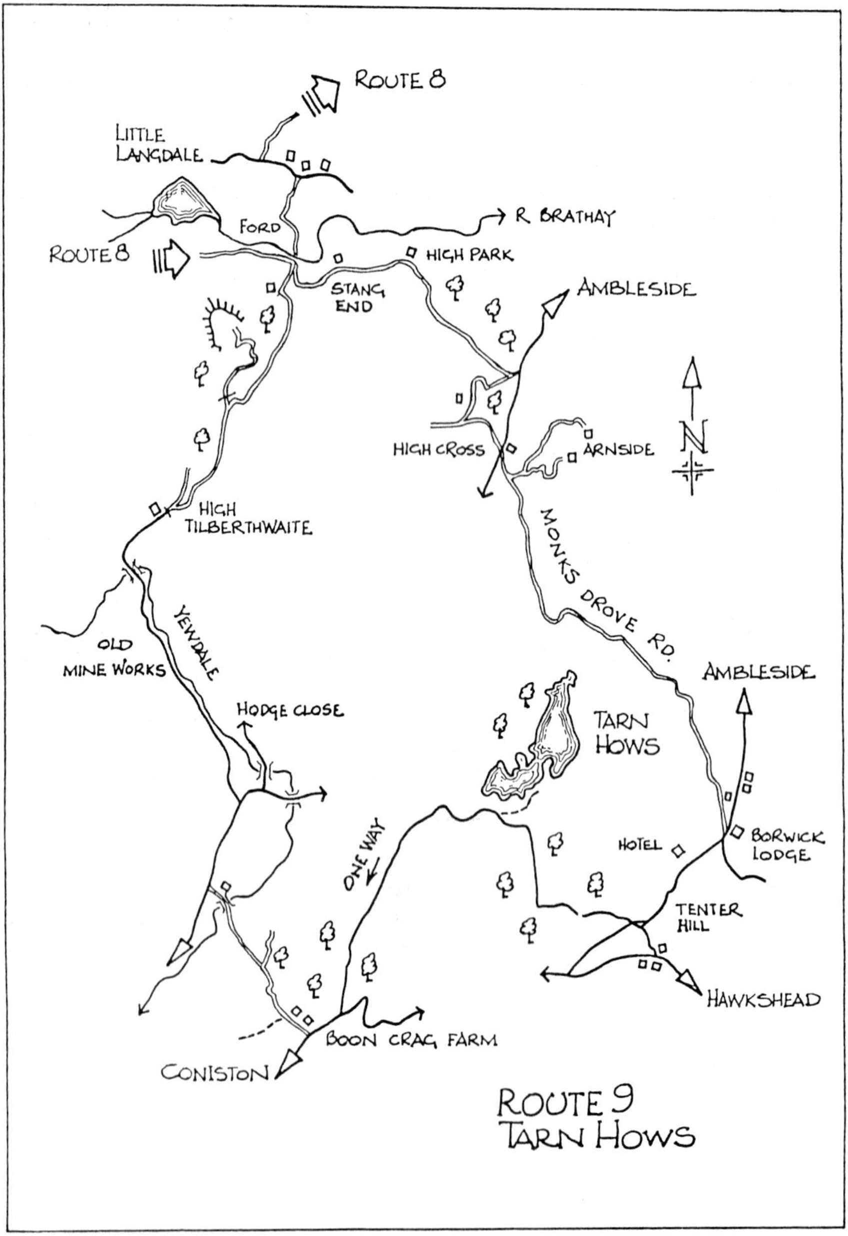
ROUTE 8
LITTLE LANGDALE
FORD
R. BRATHAY
ROUTE 8
HIGH PARK
STANG END
AMBLESIDE
N
HIGH CROSS
ARNSIDE
HIGH TILBERTHWAITE
MONKS DROVE RD.
YEWDALE
OLD MINE WORKS
AMBLESIDE
HODGE CLOSE
TARN HOWS
ONE WAY
HOTEL
BORWICK LODGE
TENTER HILL
HAWKSHEAD
BOON CRAG FARM
CONISTON
ROUTE 9
TARN HOWS

9 Tarn Hows

AS STATED at the start of Route 8, the Tarn Hows circuit is ideally suited to being combined with the Langdales to make a figure of eight pivoting about Tilberthwaite Ford. If this has been the plan then skip the next paragraph.

From Elterwater, home of Huddlestons Gunpowder Works, since departed and now the Langdale timeshare, follow the closing stages of Route 8 backwards over the bridge, past the youth hostel and up the hill to the hotel. Fork right here and left at the next one and begin a rough climb towards Little Langdale. Don't hang around for too long though, the goats have a habit of eating anything standing still! Turn left on the road and right just before the chapel to drop down steeply to the above mentioned ford — try crossing without getting boots full of water.

Heading directly away from the river and forking left almost immediately the way is, as promised in Route 2, back on the line of the Roman Road from Galava (Ambleside) to Glannoventa (Ravenglass). The exact line of the road is, as always, hard to define. A short section was excavated in 1920 a couple of hundred yards north of here and it can next be seen in the field behind Fell Foot at the bottom of Wrynose Pass which, along with Hardknott, it crosses on its way to the coast. At a later date (about 1000 years later) these same sections of road became one of the main drove roads belonging to the monks of Furness Abbey. As already mentioned, again in Chapter 2, one of the abbey's major holdings was at Brotherilkeld in Upper Eskdale and from there each winter young ewes were driven over the passes to Fell Foot, then along the lanes covered by Route 9 to Oxen Fell High Cross on what is now the main A593 Coniston road. They crossed and carried on their way along what still remains today as a wide walled road above Tarn Hows and ended their journey at the Grange at Hawkshead. At Borwick Lodge turn right along the main road and right again following the signposts to Tarn Hows.

It can be said that when a person is held in anxious suspense they are on Tenterhooks. Just another of the many cliches that slip off the tongue and nobody ever thinks of the meaning behind it. Well, look no further! When making wool cloth was still a cottage industry the finished material, once woven and washed was *stretched* between the tenter hooks and laid in the sun on the hillside to dry. The field on the left of the triangular island is still marked on the 1:25000 as maps as tenter hill.

For a halfway break, what better place than Tarn Hows? However, it hasn't always been the picturesque spot that adorns a thousand picture postcards but was in fact created by the Victorians in their search for the romantic by damming up the beck and transforming a few swampy puddles into a splendid tarn. From the car parks above Tarn Hows the lane to Coniston is a real delight. It runs steeply downhill AND is one way so nothing can suddenly appear from the opposite direction!

Upon reaching the main road turn right, and right again in 250 yards through the timber yards at Boon Crag Farm. This short bridleway crosses over into Yewdale, definitely one of the most pleasing of the small valleys and unusual in that it has a road running up both sides of the beck. The one on the far bank runs to Hodge Close Quarries and this one to Tilberthwaite Mines and Little Langdale.

The Tilberthwaite Mines are the third in a ring of workings surrounding Wetherlam, the others are Coniston Copper Mines and Greenburn (Route 8) that A. Wainwright refers to in book 4 of his pictorial guide to the lakeland fells as "Wetherlams hundred holes". As well as the shafts and levels of the above, these include the gigantic slate workings of Penny Rigg, Hodge Close and Moss Rigg, these three lying roughly in the centre of a bed of bright sea-green slate that runs from Walna Scar in the south west (Route 10) through Elterwater to Loughrigg (Route 1) and Kirkstone Pass in the north east. The slate is still finished at the cutting and polishing mill at Skelwith Bridge and is well worth a visit on a rainy day, as are the tea rooms!

At High Tilberthwaite the surface road ends and a rough quarry track giving an excellent ride to the ford begins, skirting the bottom of the Moss Rigg spoil heaps on its way. And so back at the ford again, a final attempt at crossing without falling off and follow the opening paragraphs, in reverse as usual, back to Elterwater.

10 Walna Scar

AS CONISTON WATER is the lowest of the lakes, a mere 105' above sea level and the summit of the Walna Scar Road at 1984' is the highest point in the book, then it goes without saying that there is a lot of climbing involved in Route 10. Start from opposite the petrol station on the Torver road and climb gently to the Sun Hotel, the Walna Scar is signposted from here up around the back of the old railway station. Opened in 1859, the Furness Railway's branch line from Foxfield Junction on the Duddon Estuary to Coniston provided a steady income for the village both from the pockets of the tourists and the mines of the "Old Man". Until then copper and slate had been transported down the Walna (it was Walney then) Scar to Kirkby Quay jetties by boat along the lake to Nibthwaite, by cart to Greenodd and finally by boat again to its destination — not very cost effective. The railway was eventually closed in 1957, a mere two years off its centenary, and is sadly missed by all who travelled it.

Dixon Ground is steep but better to get some of the climbing out of the way on the easier tarmac surface. The surface ends at the car park but that's already 650' of height gained, the large track heading right from here leads to the Old Man of Coniston, one of the most climbed, most defaced yet most revered of the Lakes Mountains. In half a mile or so another well used track ascends to the right; this one, however, is private and goes up to Bursting Stone (aptly named, isn't it?) Quarry, one of the few slate quarries still in production. Watch out for the huge yellow lorries that come careering down here.

Just opposite the quarry track is a small reedy puddle masquerading under the name of Boo Tarn and to the south east of this is a small circular enclosure. Excavated in 1909 by W.G. Collingwood it was proved to contain two bronze age urns both containing cremated remains and as there have been similiar discoveries in the Duddon valley just perhaps a line along the Walna Scar was walked, in the course of family reunions nearly 3000 years ago . . .

Cross Torver Beck by Cove Bridge, a superb example of a packhorse bridge, a single high arch to prevent flood damage and low parapets to allow the passage of the packs slung either side of the horses — the metal railings were added later. Now the hard work begins, a series of rock cuttings and steep zig zags leads to the top of the pass. It must have been tough because at the top is a small stone shelter for the driver to sit out of the wind.

The route now turns south along the flanks of White Pike to a gate in the intake wall where the main track drops steeply down alongside the beck to Seathwaite. Keeping to this side of the wall, turn left along the bottom of the spoil heap to meet a well graded path and where this forks in a muddy

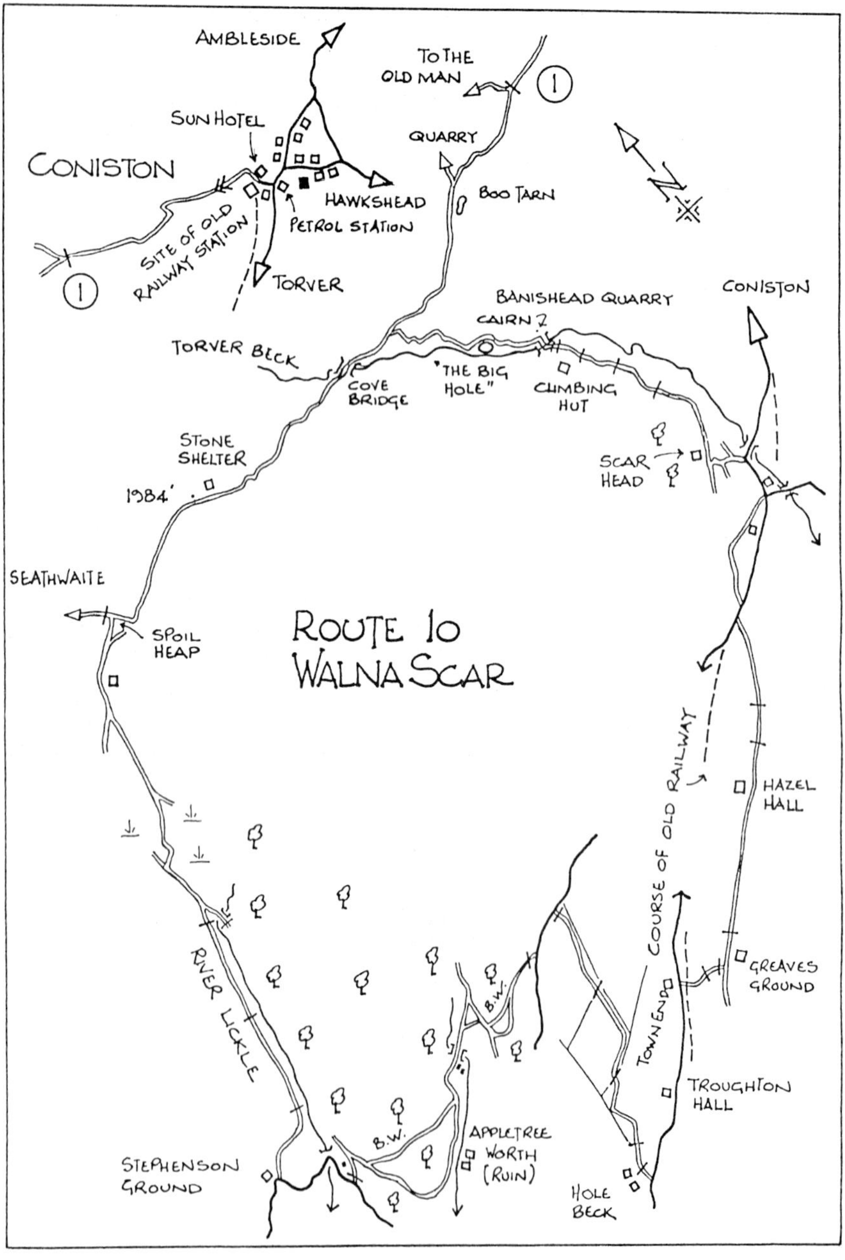
AMBLESIDE
TO THE OLD MAN
1
SUN HOTEL
CONISTON
QUARRY
BOO TARN
HAWKSHEAD
PETROL STATION
SITE OF OLD RAILWAY STATION
1
TORVER
BANISHEAD QUARRY
CONISTON
CAIRN
TORVER BECK
"THE BIG HOLE"
COVE BRIDGE
CLIMBING HUT
STONE SHELTER
SCAR HEAD
1984'
SEATHWAITE
SPOIL HEAP
ROUTE 10 WALNA SCAR
COURSE OF OLD RAILWAY
HAZEL HALL
RIVER LICKLE
GREAVES GROUND
B.W.
TOWNEND
TROUGHTON HALL
B.W.
APPLETREE WORTH (RUIN)
STEPHENSON GROUND
HOLE BECK

quarter of a mile, take the upper branch to the left. This way follows an easy grassy terrace which deteriorates as it goes, at one point a better track, embanked in places with stones, heading up to the left. Don't go this way but angle down right through a bad swamp to rejoin the main track on the other side of the beck. Recently a line of blue flags marked the way from here along the splendid bridleway to Stephenson Ground, however, as they may only be temporary it follows the right hand side of the valley keeping the forest on the left.

The steepest section of the Walna Scar. *(Dave Lee)*

The names Stephenson Ground and that of its neighbour Jackson Ground originate form a treaty signed in 1509 between the monks of Furness Abbey and the "squatters" on their land, Mr. Stephenson and Mr. Jackson included. Each tenant was given the right to enclose land up to 1½ acres and to build a farmhouse on that land subject to the payment of a yearly rent to the abbot. The enclosures or grounds usually took the name of the new owner and over 20 can still be found in High Furness today.

After crossing the River Lickle at Water Yeat Bridge continue along the road for a hundred yards or so before turning left through a gate into the forest. Here the usual Forestry Commission pattern applies. There are Forest Roads and Bridleways but the two seldom coincide. The bridleways were marked by the same blue flags as earlier but, just in case, both are shown on the map. If all goes well and the road is reached then follow it left 200 yards and then go through the gate on the right into a grassy field. Bear left to meet the wall (the walls are shown on the map to help here as it is fairly complicated) and follow its length, through one gate until a crosswall coming from back left is encountered. Without crossing, follow this to the right, go through the next gate on the left and head downhill, keeping the wall in sight to meet the main road at Hole Beck. Opposite Town End cottage a short length of farm track crosses the old railway bed and meets a narrow lane at Greaves Ground, this leads to Torver. Passing through the village at a triangular island a lane leads up to Scar Head where bearing right join the old climbers track to Dow Crags. Up to the new climbing hut there is a reasonable surface but from there to the Walna Scar is a real mixture. Keep to the right of the hut between a wall and a fence until a complex sheep fold is reached. Pass through the first two gates into the second enclosure and then turn right to exit and cross the footbridge over Torver beck, a slate sign propped up by a slate pillar points the way. On coming out from between the two spoil heaps of Bannishead Quarry an amazing sight meets the eye. One of the old slate pits is flooded, the water is an indescribable shade of blue and on the far side part of the beck cascades into the depths. All that remains now is to zig zag up the grassy bank towards the nick in the skyline, catch a breath and head off back down to Coniston, twice as fast as coming up the same way this morning.

11 Skiddaw House

NOT MANY people visit the "Back o'Skidda" these days, yet it is a landscape so totally at odds with the rest of the Lake District that it deserves a look if only to satisfy the curiosity. The explanation is a simple one. Geologically, Lakeland is split into three. Below a line joining Coniston, Ambleside and Shap, where most of the previous routes lie, the rock is a succession of sedimentary layers, Brathay Flags, Coniston Grits and Bannisdale Slates giving the easy going terrain of Claife Heights and Grizedale. Above this, but to the south of a second line joining Ennerdale, Buttermere and the southern end of Derwentwater, is the Lakeland core, the tough Borrowdale volcanics forming the Scafells, Langdales, Helvellyn and High Street. Finally, and this is where we're heading, to the north are the Skiddaw Slates, oldest of the lot, an area of bleak rolling moorland and deserted valleys rich in minerals and wildlife, yet virtually unchanged since Brigantian tribesmen gazed down from their fortress on Carrock Fell.

To find the way out of Keswick, ask for the Cumberland Pencil Works, everybody knows where it is — it's been there since 1832 and originally used black lead or Plumbago from the Borrowdale mines on the slopes of Grey Knotts. The main road turns left following the river to pass through the "suburb" of Crossthwaite and this may have been the original Keswick before the railway brought the tourists in 1865 and that end of town expanded rapidly. Crossthwaite is first mentioned in AD 590 as the clearing (Norse = thwaite) where St. Kentigern planted his cross and preached to the locals and even now the Parish Church of Keswick at Crossthwaite is dedicated to him, as are seven others in northern Lakeland.

At the large roundabout on the A66 take the second exit, the A591 to Bothel but turn right after only a hundred yards along the lane to Applethwaite. Pass the front entrance to the Underscar Hotel and then backtrack at the next junction along Gale Road to pass the rear of the same on the way to the car park behind Latrigg — this bit is very steep!

There is an alternative "off road" route to the car park from behind the railway station but it is quite hard going and as it is on the main route to Skiddaw, in summer is very busy. The road route is probably quicker if slightly longer.

Through a gate at the end of the car park pass along a "lane" between a wall and a fence, very narrow and quite tricky if the bikes have mark I extra wide handlebars. Emerging from the gate at the other end of the lane the track splits, the left fork going to Skiddaw summit. Those who wish to cycle all the way to the top, 3053', can do so legally, the view from the cairn is superb and the race back down magnificent.

If going this way, pause a while at the Hawell monument to reflect on the epitaph, "Great Shepherd of thy heavenly flock, These men have left our hill, Their feet were on the living rock, Oh guide and bless them still." Simple words with deep meanings.

The way to Skidda' House, however, drops sharply right to Whit Beck, through the ford and then along a beautiful grassy terrace to suddenly turn a corner around Lonscale Crags and face us with an amazing sight. Gone are the gentle slopes and views of Derwentwater, here is a narrow rocky path hewn out of the mountainside and a drop of over 600′ to the Glenderaterra Beck — wow! Continue along this seemingly precarious ledge for just on a mile until it drops to join another track coming up from the beck on the right — this is the way home, so remember it just in case the clouds come down. Looking down in the valley notice the track following the beck to end amongst a group of derelict buildings. This is, or rather was, the Brundholme Mine, dating from the nineteenth century and one of the many offshoots of the lead workings of the Blencathra group based around Woodend near Threlkeld. Keep above the wall until a gate and stile is reached and there, perched on the hillside, defying the elements with only a windbent stand of conifers for protection, is Skidda' House.

The house was originally built as shepherds' cottages but since the last one moved out it has been both an Outdoor Pursuits Centre and a Youth Hostel. Now it stands empty again keeping a watchful eye on the Caldew and awaiting its next tenants.

To get back to Keswick return to the junction mentioned earlier, drop down to the left to cross the Glenderaterra and a superb tracks leads down to the Blencathra Centre in a fraction of the time it took to get up to Skidda' House. The new National Park Centre has served time as both a sanatorium and an isolation hospital before finding its present vocation.

Unfortunately the bridleways are now over but a route around Keswick would not be complete without a visit to Castlerigg Stone Circle.

Upon crossing the main A66 the hat-trick of the Lakes' Roman Roads will have been completed. The southern route from Kendal to Ravenglass (Routes 1, 4 and 9), High Street (Routes 4 and 5) and now the Northern Route from Old Penrith five miles north of "New" Penrith to Papcastle near Cockermouth. From Old Penrith to the multiple camps at Troutbeck (GR 384273) the line of the road is reasonably clear and similarly from Braithwaite over the Whinlatter Pass to Papcastle, the only grey area is around Keswick. Calculated guesses based on small facts point to there being a Roman Fort at Castlerigg itself. Now that would be an interesting find.

The "Druids Circle" is a fascinating place — although no-one has come up with a definite reason for the stones. Many theories involving astronomical and religious thoughts have been brought forward but one thing rarely mentioned is this — If you draw a line from the summits of Skiddaw and Helvellyn and then do the same from Blencathra to High Spy they cross exactly at Castlerigg. Coincidence? I don't think so, but as to the reason . . .?

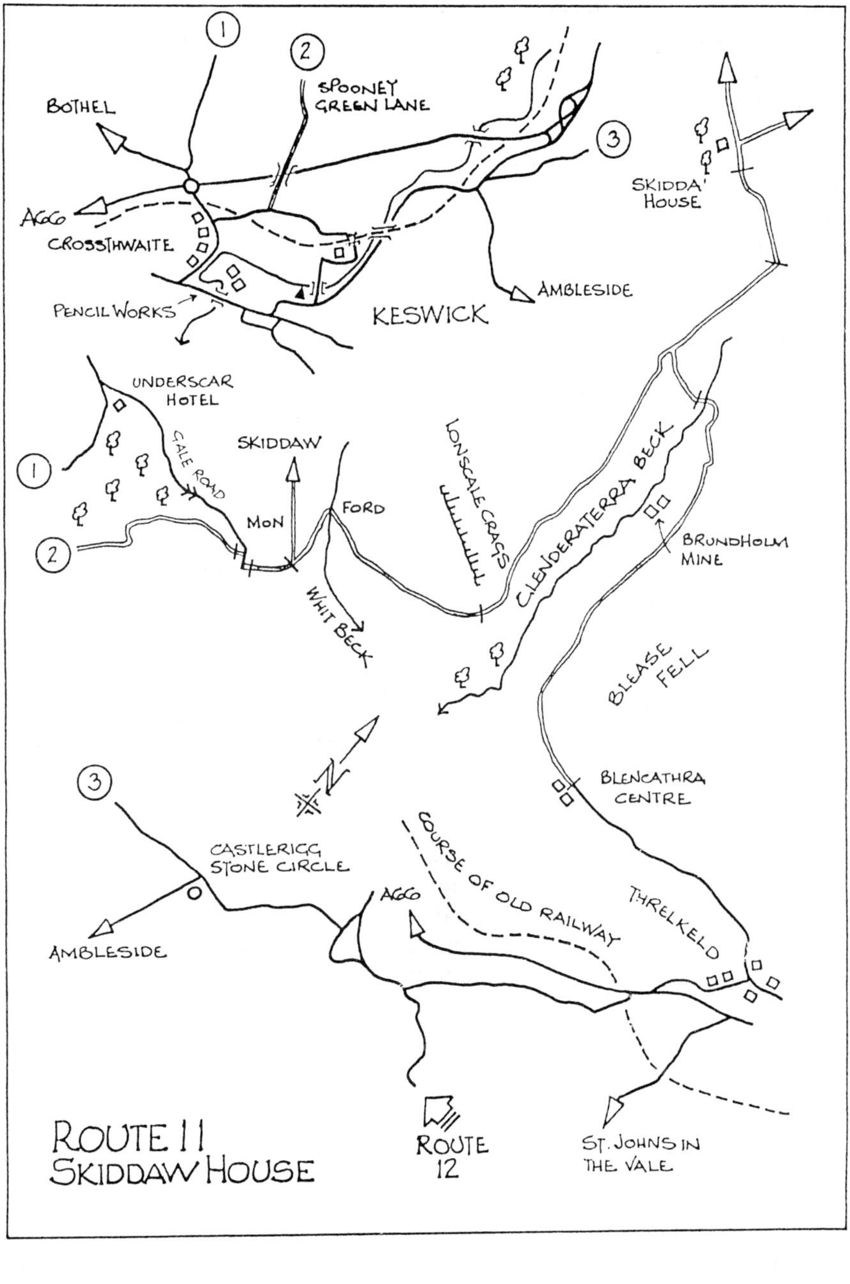

1
2
SPOONEY GREEN LANE
BOTHEL
3
SKIDDA' HOUSE
A66
CROSSTHWAITE
AMBLESIDE
PENCIL WORKS
KESWICK
UNDERSCAR HOTEL
GALE ROAD
SKIDDAW
LONSCALE CRAGS
GLENDERATERRA BECK
1
MON
FORD
BRUNDHOLM MINE
2
WHIT BECK
BLEASE FELL
N
3
BLENCATHRA CENTRE
COURSE OF OLD RAILWAY
CASTLERIGG STONE CIRCLE
A66
THRELKELD
AMBLESIDE
ROUTE 12
ST. JOHNS IN THE VALE
ROUTE 11
SKIDDAW HOUSE

12 Moor Divock

ROUTE 12, tucked away as it is in the far North Eastern corner of the Lake District is not the most accessible route in the book. However, it is a particular favourite of mine and it is handy if you happen to be staying in Penrith!

For the last reason alone the way around will be described as a figure of eight from Askham, half an hour at the most from Penrith town centre. Askham is a most interesting village having both ancient cottages combined with blocks of houses that would go unnoticed on a Birmingham housing estate. To leave the village, take the dead end lane opposite the pub and the post office to the end of town and a cattle grid with one bar missing, very tricky. Through the gate keep close to the wall on the right until a second gate is reached in just over half a mile. The wall that has been followed suddenly heads right here and if nowhere else (especially if misty) a compass bearing on the cairn at the crossroads is vital. Moor Divock is a desolate place, don't end up on the summit of Heughscar Hill as I once did!

At the junction, a four way signpost points to Pooley Bridge, Helton, Askham and Howtown. Take the latter, still on the same bearing, over an indistinct and extremely boggy section of track to reach the Cockpit, maybe in later years the site of illegal wagering but undoubtedly built many centuries before with other aims in mind. As the Stone Age matured into bronze so the population of the villages in the Eden Valley and Cumbria's Western shore grew until a time came when new sites had to be found. The people turned their attention to the higher ground and settled in three main areas namely, West Cumberland around Burnmoor and Ennerdale, Furness (Route 10) and Crosby Ravensworth and its semi-permanent satellite, Moor Divock. The mother settlement on Crosby Ravensworth was so important that the Roman Road from Carlisle to Lancaster seems to make a detour to pass within 20 yards of it.

After fording Elder Beck the way becomes clearer as it flanks Arthurs Pike on its descent to Howtown. Cross Aik Beck in a deep ravine and then head for the wall above the trees on the right. At one point the sound of rushing water can be heard, this is coming from one of the inspection chambers on the Hayeswater aqueduct, a small part of the network of pipelines connecting the reservoirs of Thirlmere, Haweswater and Hayeswater ultimately to provide water for Manchester.

At Swarthbeck, double back through the gate marked with the blue bridleway arrow and pass through the stables to the shore road to Pooley Bridge.

If whilst cycling a route anybody ventures to complain about the damage Mountain Bikes do to the paths try politely suggesting they come and have a

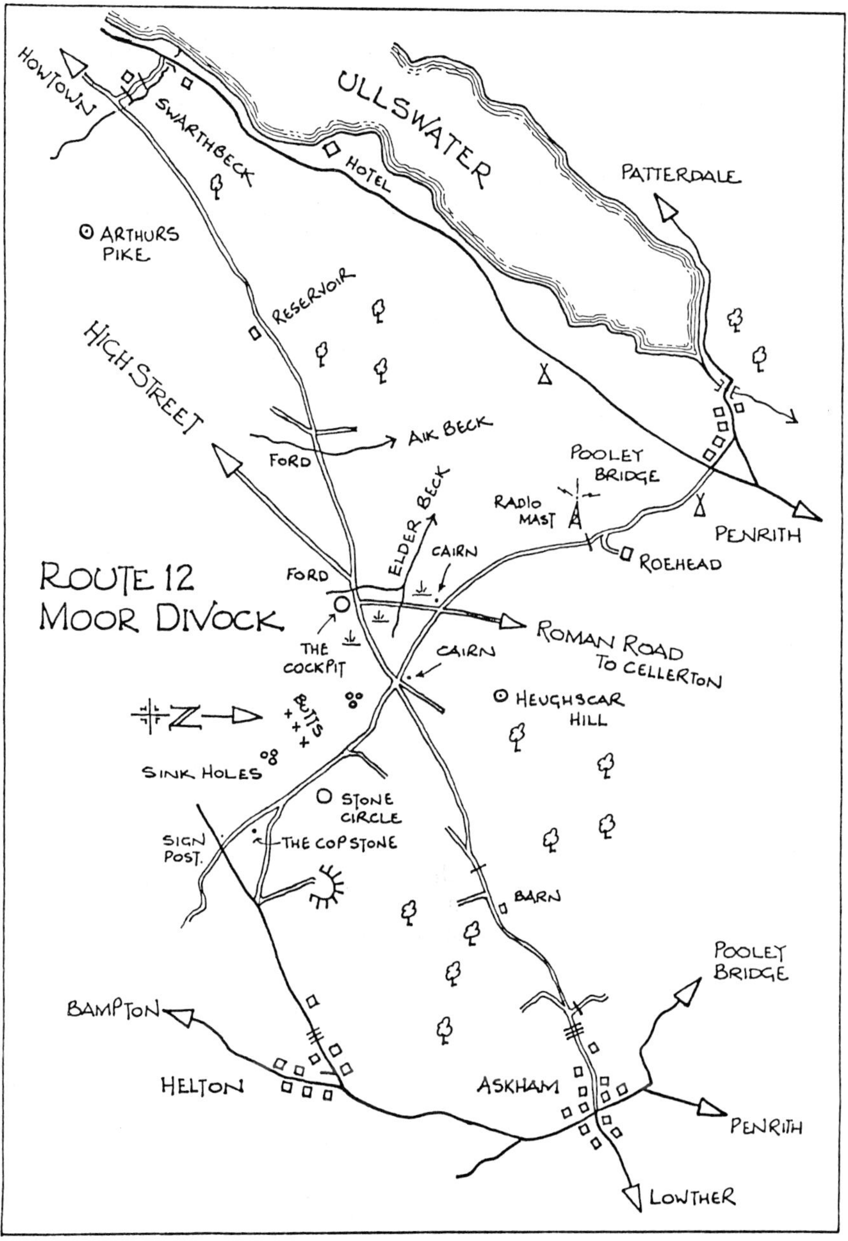

ROUTE 12
MOOR DIVOCK
ULLSWATER
HOWTOWN
SWARTHBECK
HOTEL
PATTERDALE
ARTHURS PIKE
RESERVOIR
HIGH STREET
AIK BECK
FORD
POOLEY BRIDGE
RADIO MAST
ELDER BECK
PENRITH
CAIRN
ROEHEAD
FORD
THE COCKPIT
ROMAN ROAD TO CELLERTON
CAIRN
HEUGHSCAR HILL
BUTTS
SINK HOLES
STONE CIRCLE
SIGN POST.
THE COPSTONE
BARN
POOLEY BRIDGE
BAMPTON
HELTON
ASKHAM
PENRITH
LOWTHER

The crossroads on Moor Divock. *(Mike Hyde)*

look around here and see what total annihilation horses, the riders of which always get a friendly wave, do to the same.

The road along the lakeside is easy going and Pooley Bridge will be reached in a matter of minutes. If a lunch break is not required, turn right at the crossroads and along the lane to Roehead. Here, especially in winter, the semi-wild fell ponies gather to be fed. These animals roam Moor Divock, mixing with the sheep and it is not unusual to find the two huddled together behind a wall to shelter from the wind. Navigation on this half of the figure eight is exceptionally straightforward, the path running in a virtually straight line from end to end and passing numerous landmarks on the way. Historians are not sure of the origins of this highway although most agree it is very ancient. One theory is that it is a section of a link between the hill fort on Dunmallet, the wooded mound behind Pooley Bridge and the avenue of standing stones at Shap.

At the first cairn the Roman Road from Brougham over High Street to Troutbeck is crossed and signposted and at the second the same is done with the first half of the route. Now, on the right of the track, as it descends to the unfenced lane to Helton are the Pulpit and Wofa Holes. These water eroded shake holes are a dead giveaway that this is limestone country. Finally on the left are more bronze age relics, a small cairn burial circle and the Cop Stone, a large upended boulder thought to be an ancient signpost. Once the lane is met, turn left to Helton and left again on the main road to return to the starting point at Askham.

Some Cycle Shops in and around the Lake District

Arragons Cycle Centre, 2 Brunswick Road, Penrith	0768 890344
Ashtons Cycle Centre, 12 Main Road, Windermere	05394 47779
Askew Cycle Centre, Kent Works, Burneside Road, Kendal	0539 728057
Biketreks, The Old Post House, Millans Park, Ambleside	05394 31245
Brucies Bike Shop, 9 Kirkland, Kendal	0539 727230
Derwent Cycles, 4 Market Place, Cockermouth	0900 822113
Ghyllside Cycles, The Slack, Ambleside	05394 33592
Halfords, 54 Stricklandgate, Kendal	0539 720467
Harper Cycles, 1-2 Middlegate, Penrith	0768 64475
Keswick Mountain Bike Centre, Southey Mill Lane, Keswick	07687 75202
Lakeland Leisure, The Chalet, Station Precinct, Windermere	05394 44786
Wheelbase, Staveley Mill Yard, Staveley, Kendal	0539 821443
Whiteheads, 35 King Street, Penrith	0768 62910
Windermere Cycle Centre, South Terrace, Bowness-on-Windermere	05394 44479

Some Hire Centres in and around the Lake District

Ambleside Mountain Bikes, Waterhead, Ambleside	05394 32014
Bike Treks, Rothay Holme Ind. Estate, Ambleside	05394 31245
Grizedale Mountain Bikes, Old Hall Car Park, Grizedale	0229 860369
Lakeland Leisure, The Chalet, Station Precinct, Windermere	05394 44786
Summittreks, 14 Yewdale Road, Coniston	05394 41212
Windermere Cycle Centre, South Terrace, Bowness-on-Windermere	05394 44479

A Short Bibliography

Hardyment C., *Arthur Ransome and Captain Flint's Trunk* (Johnathan Cape, 1984).
Hindle B.P., *Roads and Trackways of the Lake District* (Moorland, 1984).
The Lake District National Park (H.M.S.O., 1975).
Leferbure M., *Cumbrian Discovery* (Gollancz, 1977).
Marshall J.D. & Davies-Shiel M., *Industrial Archaeology of the Lake Counties* (Scolar Press, 1969).
Millward R. & Robinson A., *Cumbria* (Macmillan, 1972).
Nicholson N., *Portrait of the Lakes* (Robert Hale, 1963).
Orrell R., *Saddle Tramp in the Lake District* (Robert Hale, 1979).
Postlethwaite, J., *Mines and Mining in the English Lake District* (Moon, 1877).
Rollinson W., *A History of Man in the Lake District* (Dent, 1967).
Rollinson W., *A History of Cumberland and Westmorland* (Phillimore, 1978).
Sale R. & Lees A., *The Ancient Ways of the Lake District* (Deutsch, 1986).
Shaw W.T., *Mining in the Lake Counties* (Dalesman, 1970).
Taylor C.D., *Portrait of Windermere* (Robert Hale, 1983).
Wainwright A., *A Pictorial Guide to the Lakeland Fells* (Westmorland Gazette, 1955–1966).
Williams L.A., *Road Transport in Cumbria in the 19th century* (Allen & Unwin, 1975).
Wyatt J., *Reflections on the Lakes* (W.H. Allen, 1980).